## ONE MAN'S JOURNEY

# GRACE
# FOR THE
# BATTLE
# OF MY LIFE

There is always
HOPE! Psalm 23

**StMarq** *Media*

One Man's Journey, Grace For The Fight Of My Life
Copyright © 2021 by Steve Marquez

ISBN: 978-1-365-52773-9

StMarq Media • 10362 Cole Road • Whittier, CA 90603

www.stmarq.com

*To my dearest, loveliest Monica, whose love and support have been the very hands and feet of God in my life. To say I am grateful is an understatement. I praise God daily that he has brought her into my life.*

*Thank you to the doctors and nurses that have quite literally saved my life.*

*Special thanks to Margot Bass, who read through my early manuscripts and made crucial changes that allowed me to continue to make this book a reality. Thank you to all who read the early copies and gave me your input as well. You are the best!*

*Most especially, thank you to my Lord and Savior, Jesus Christ, who gave his life to save mine. Some how, Thank you, does not seem to be enough.*

# TABLE OF CONTENTS

# PROLOGUE

In April of 2014, I was diagnosed with stage 3, Renal Cell Carcinoma (RCC), which is kidney cancer. Then later, was diagnosed with stage4. I knelt beside my wife, who was laying in bed, and we cried and prayed and prayed and cried. Next, I gathered my sons, Cody, Jared and Andrew together and told them the news. We cried together and I tried to answer as many questions as possible to the best of my ability.

## THIS IS MY STORY.

## MATTHEW 8:23-27

"Now when He got into a boat, His disciples followed Him. And suddenly a great tempest arose on the sea, so that the boat was covered with the waves. But He was asleep. Then His disciples came to Him and awoke Him, saying, "Lord, save us! We are perishing!" But He said to them, "Why are you fearful, O you of little faith?" Then He arose and rebuked the winds and the sea, and there was a great calm. So the men marveled, saying, "Who can this be, that even the winds and the sea obey Him?"

# MARK 4:34-41

"On the same day, when evening had come, He said to them, "Let us cross over to the other side." Now when they had left the multitude, they took Him along in the boat as He was. And other little boats were also with Him. And a great windstorm arose, and the waves beat into the boat, so that it was already filling. But He was in the stern, asleep on a pillow. And they awoke Him and said to Him, "Teacher, do You not care that we are perishing?" Then He arose and rebuked the wind, and said to the sea, "Peace, be still!" And the wind ceased and there was a great calm. But He said to them, "Why are you so fearful? How is it that you have no faith?" And they feared exceedingly, and said to one another, "Who can this be, that even the wind and the sea obey Him!"

# LUKE 8:22-25

"Now it happened, on a certain day, that He got into a boat with His disciples. And He said to them, "Let us cross over to the other side of the lake." And they launched out. But as they sailed He fell asleep. And a windstorm came down on the lake, and they were filling with water, and were in jeopardy. And they came to Him and awoke Him, saying, "Master, Master, we are perishing!" Then He arose and rebuked the wind and the raging of the water. And they ceased, and there was a calm. But He said to them, "Where is your faith?" And they were afraid, and marveled, saying to one another, "Who can this be? For He commands even the winds and water, and they obey Him!"

# PSALM 107:23-30

"Those who go down to the sea in ships, Who do business on great waters, They see the works of the Lord, And His wonders in the deep. For He commands and raises the stormy wind, Which lifts up the waves of the sea. They mount up to the heavens, They go down again to the depths; Their soul melts because of trouble. They reel to and fro, and stagger like a drunken man, And are at their wits' end. Then they cry out to the Lord in their trouble, And He brings them out of their distresses. He calms the storm, So that its waves are still. Then they are glad because they are quiet; So He guides them to their desired haven."

# 1.
# ROUGH SEAS AHEAD
## A RISING STORM

There were rough seas ahead. Mark and Luke say that Jesus told the disciples that they would make it to the other side. Even though the seas would be tumultuous, they would survive and, in fact, thrive.

As the storm arose outside of the boat, an even bigger one raged inside the boat; a storm of fear and confusion. I am sure when they saw the clouds, felt the wind and the first drop of rain, it wasn't a concern for them. They were in the boat. They could look to the stern and see the blanket-covered figure of the Savior getting some much needed sleep. They knew that as long as they could see Jesus, everything would be okay.

The wind became fierce and waves started crashing violently against the boat, turning the small vessel this way and that. The first wave to break over the bow must have terrified them as the boards began to creak and bend. Still, they looked to Jesus.

In my mind, I see Matthew and Simon, the Zealot, holding on tighter with each toss and turn. Matthew was a tax collector, Simon, a radical insurgent. From their profession, I gather that they were unaccustomed to the ways of the sea. The only ones on the boat who remained calm were Peter, James, John and perhaps, Andrew. They had a fishing business and knew what to do in situations like this. They weren't frightened until the wind tore at the sails and the little boat almost capsized. The other disciples' feigned calm turned to terror when Peter's normal hubris was now replaced with a look of fear. My God! We're going to drown! they must have thought. Hope was gone. Jesus was in the boat, but He was sleeping, and doing nothing.

Didn't Jesus care about their lives? That the disciples' eventually woke the soundly sleeping Savior showed they believed He could save them. But why didn't He already know that they needed rescue?

Perhaps they thought Jesus would survive because He was the Messiah and Messiahs don't die. They likely concluded that Jesus didn't care about them and was only concerned about slipping in some shuteye.

It is a terrible feeling. Knowing that the Savior is just feet away and not believing that He cares enough to save you. Thoughts like these can lead to depression and doubt. Does God love me? If Yes, then why won't He do something? If No, then I am doomed. Maybe God loves me, but I did something—some sort of horrible sin—and therefore, this storm has arisen and is the means of my undoing. Is it possible? Anything is ... in my own head.

The disciples were in the boat being tossed to and fro. Can you see them? They could see the waves overwhelm them and hear death calling out to them from the sea. They begin to view/regard/consider Jesus as a less potent Savior: Their thoughts move from a potent to an impotent Savior: Is it possible that Jesus can't save? When will He wake up and save us? If He is powerless over the storm, then, at the very least, He needs to wake up and panic like the rest of us!

There is another story in the scriptures that comes to mind when we think of a boat filled with sailors, a strong storm at sea and a sleeping prophet. It is the story of Jonah. Instead of doing what God called him to do, Jonah ran away to the sea. From the port in Joppa, he boarded a ship that was headed to the farthest reaches of civilization. A storm arose on the sea. The men were frantic, looking for any way to save themselves, even becoming instantly religious and praying to any god that would listen. As they prayed, they realized that someone was missing. It was Jonah. They searched the ship and found him below deck ... sleeping.

Jesus, like Jonah, was asleep. I am sure the disciples recalled this story. They may have thought that at the very least, Jesus should wake up and pray. Perhaps they thought a moment about throwing Him over. It is amazing how quickly we throw Him out of the boat when we are in trouble! Jesus once said that He and Jonah were similar. As Jonah was in the belly of the great fish for three days and three nights, so will the Son of Man be in the heart of the earth for three days and three nights (Matthew 12:39-41). Jonah's "sacrifice" allowing the sailors to throw him overboard brought peace and calm to the seas. Jesus' true sacrifice on the cross brought peace and calm to a world of sinners. But that is where the comparison ends. Jonah was only a prophet; Jesus, the Savior.

The disciples ran to their sleeping friend in the back of the boat to shake him out of slumber.

# DOING BUSINESS WITH GOD

*Those who go down to the sea in ships, who do business on great waters, they see the works of the Lord, and His wonders in the deep (Psalm 107:23–24).*

Those who do business see the works of the Lord. In the ancient world, the sea represented a dangerous place where there was a good chance that if you went out, you would not come back. In fact, it was where the prophet said God hides our sins—He will again have compassion on us, and will subdue our iniquities. You will cast all our sins into the depths of the sea (Micah 7:19).

The sea did not symbolize a place of pleasure where people went for fun or relaxation. They were serious sailors doing serious business. It was these sailors of whom the Psalmist is speaking. They were on a mission. Usually it had to do with trade, exploration for gold or as ambassadors, like Solomon's sailors (1 Kings 10:22) or those who were in the employ of kings Jehoshaphat (1 Kings 22:48) and Ahaziah (2 Chronicles 20:35-37). They were the ones who saw the works of the LORD.

The works of the Lord are the storms that would arise on the sea. It is one thing to be in a storm on land where there are places to shelter: a nice cave, somewhere underground or even a well-built structure. But to be on the sea represented unthinkable dangers. There was nowhere to run as ships would rise and then run down the back side of large swells. It was a marvel of the ancient world that they could survive such punishment. In fact, seeing this "act of God"—His awesome destructive power— would terrify them.

Sailors are as superstitious as baseball players. Seeing the hand of God, they would figure out what they could do to appease His anger and calm the sea.

# MY STORY

In April of 2014, I was diagnosed with stage 3, Renal Cell Carcinoma (RCC), which is kidney cancer. I had been experiencing fevers since January 14, and I was fatigued. Originally, we had thought it was some sort of parasite I picked up while on a missions trip to Cambodia in 2013. But after some tests, doctors determined that I had a 7-cm tumor on my kidney and possibly in the vena cava, a main artery to the lower part of the body; they were going to determine if it was operable. My doctor called me later to confirm the diagnosis of cancer. My wife, Monica, and I held hands. I knelt beside the bed, and we cried and prayed and prayed and cried. Next, I gathered my sons, Cody, Jared and Andrew together and told them the news. We cried together and I tried to answer as many questions as possible to the best of my ability.

I had the first operation in Dallas on July 1, 2014. Doctors determined that the tumor had not entered into the vena cava (although tumor thrombus, or blood clots, were present), nor had the cancer spread anywhere else in the body. I was on the mend, and everything looked great.

# ORDINARY DAY

I had no idea of the journey that I would face after going back to normal life. A storm like none other was about to rise in my life that would shake me to the core.

After eight weeks, I went back to work. I started feeling fatigued again. In fact, at one point, I fell asleep at my desk at work. Eventually, the fevers returned and my left leg started getting numb, like it was falling asleep. We weren't really sure what it was but wanted to check it out. My primary care physician referred me to my oncologist, who set up a bone scan on October 24th to see if the cancer was active again. The night before the scan, as I was changing and lifted up my right leg, my left leg gave out, and I fell on my back. It was one of the most excruciating feelings of pain I had experienced to that point. I tried to lay and rest a bit to see if it would go away. It didn't. My wife Monica wanted me to go to the hospital, but I wouldn't go. I don't know what it is about men, but we like to writhe in pain for a while before actually doing something about it. Eventually, the pain overwhelmed me and, after a while, we went to the ER.

The Emergency Room, now called the Emergency Department, was what you would expect. A white tiled floor and fluorescent lights in the ceiling that brought a certain coldness to the place. There was a carpeted part of the room to the left of the front desk filled with chairs and about 10 people who were sick, injured or otherwise in need of emergency medical attention. My wife helped me through the automatic sliding doors and into a wheelchair. I went up to the desk while she parked the car. I was still in a lot of pain when the nurse asked the nature of my visit.

I told them I was a cancer patient and had fallen, and thought I had injured my back from the fall. After a bit, I was given a CT scan and we were led to another, more private, waiting room. I remember laying in a stretcher, Monica in a seat a few feet from me when the ER physician entered the room with the results. The doctor said, "Mr. Marquez, you don't have a back problem, your cancer has returned." He said that there was a 6-cm tumor in my spine that had grown back in about three months. After he left to begin paperwork to have me admitted to the hospital, I looked over at Monica and said, "I wonder if I'll be here for Christmas?" We both cried.

I now had stage 4, metastatic RCC. I was placed in a room overnight and then the next morning was told I would be going to a hospital by ambulance. I remember being put into the back of the ambulance and getting strapped in and the paramedic looking toward the driver and asking if he was okay to drive. He was just at the end of an all night shift. I remember him saying that all he needed was his tunes! Well, let's just say we "drove by Braille" for two and a half hours until we reached CHI St. Vincents Infirmary in Little Rock, AR. The first surgery was in July, and now, in October, I figured the cancer was so aggressive it would be unstoppable.

# FAITH IS NECESSARY

*For He commands and raises the stormy wind, which lifts up the waves of the sea. They mount up to the heavens, they go down again to the depths; their soul melts because of trouble (Psalm 107:25–26).*

The disciples' boat began to fill with water, and they were concerned that they would be killed as the boat sunk. I felt the same way. Cancer, like the water in that boat, was filling my spine, muscles and nerves.

St. Vincent's Infirmary in Little Rock, Arkansas was the first in-state a hospital that could handle my kind of problem with a bed available. It was a great blessing that I went there. I was placed in a room in the NSICU and met Dr. Stephen Shafizadeh, my neurosurgeon. He discussed different options with me and said that he would get a team of doctors together to come up with a plan in the next few days. Later, he told me that he was looking for a surgeon who would get him to my spine so he could remove the cancer from my body.

We looked at the medical records and found where the general surgeon—who eventually took the job—

explained to me that the risk for this kind of surgery was high. He expected me to die in surgery. My general surgeon stated: "The risk and complications were discussed with him (Steve) in detail, including postoperative bleeding, infection, and numerous other possible complications regarding this 'big undertaking.' 'Consent to surgery stated 'decline of condition and death.'"

I was put into physical rehabilitation for a few days to get strong enough for the upcoming surgeries. I would have three:

The first on November 7, 2014, to embolize the tumor to keep me from bleeding to death. It took 5.5 hours.

The second was on November 10, 2014, going through the left flank, working on the front, removing tumor from my spine, nerves and psoas muscle. Dr. Shafizadeh scraped the cancer off the nerves as one of his partners, Dr. Raja, held them. They also removed two of my vertebrae, L-2, L-3, and placed a cage in their place. During the surgery, they had to collapse my lung in order to reach the area affected by cancer. It took 7.5 hours.

The third surgery was on November 18, 2014, placing metal rods and screws on my spine from T-10 to my pelvis. All three surgeries were within 11 days. The surgeries were so long that another pastor told me that he expected that Monica would post on Facebook that "Steve had gone home to be with the Lord." It took 10 hours.

To put it into perspective, that is twenty-three hours of surgery in eleven days!

# IS GOD ASLEEP?

*They reel to and fro, and stagger like a drunken man, and are at their wits' end. Then they cry out to the Lord in their trouble, and He brings them out of their distresses (Psalm 107:27–28).*

The disciples went to Jesus, whom they still found asleep, and woke Him. He got up, rebuked the wind and the raging sea and there was an immediate calm.

It is not clear if Jesus rebuked the wind and the sea first, or if he asked about their faith first.

Why does this stand out to me? Because it is different every time. Sometimes God asks us to trust him BEFORE He changes our circumstances. Other times, He asks us why we couldn't trust Him AFTER He changes our circumstances. For me, it was definitely BEFORE. I needed to trust Him before my circumstances would change.

When I came out of surgery, I experienced an incredible amount of darkness, the like I had never before experienced. The Lord had never left me, but it was as if He said, "This is what you would be like without me without My light." I hated the feeling. It was terrifying. Usually you experience difficulties like this as a believer and expect to go through it singing and praising the Lord the whole time. But I didn't. I was extremely fearful. I had never thought of myself as a fearful person, but I was terrified. I sought the Lord, but nothing seemed to help except Monica's presence in the room.

You never get sleep in the hospital. I don't know what it is about nurses, but they always seem to want to wake you up at 4am. Because of my collapsed lung, they had to do daily X-Rays of my lungs to make sure they were filling properly. I also had to do breathing exercises. The X-rRay machine must have come from the children's area because it was shaped like a giraffe, with spots all over; it had a large base, its body, a neck with a head, which pointed at me to take the X-Ray. It looked just like a giraffe! They would wheel it in, then would have to put a film board behind me in the bed, which straightened my back and caused me an enormous amount of pain. Sadly, I fought the nurses, which made me strain my muscles even more and caused additional pain. Every morning I would wake up and ask the nurse, "Do they have to bring the giraffe in today?" She would look at me kind of puzzled, then at Monica, who would say, "Oh, he's talking about the X-Ray machine." The nurses would laugh!

There is much more, but after my time in the NSICU and the floor of the hospital I was released to a physical therapy hospital in Fort Smith, Arkansas. I remember the day I was released. I said, "Praise the

Lord!" The assisting neurosurgeon, who happened to be doing rounds that morning, responded, "Oh, yes, praise the Lord. I told your wife, 'It was not us who did this surgery, it was too complex. There was an angel in the room that did it.'" They were amazed at how well I was doing.

# THE WIND AND SEA REBUKED

Jesus asked his disciples why their faith was so small. When they heard Jesus and saw the calm sea, they were amazed! They knew Him as a great teacher and even the King of the Jews, the Messiah, but they did not realize the authority He had over nature.

I started getting better. The winds were dying down and slowly, I was realizing the miracle that God had done in me.

I was at the rehabilitation hospital for almost a week, beginning in a wheelchair, unable to walk steadily, then moving to a walker. I was released to six months of outpatient physical therapy. I remember at one of my appointments Dr. Shafizadeh asked me to walk around the room a bit. I went for the door of the exam room to walk in the hallway, but he didn't want me to overexert myself. I walked a bit in the room and then he opened the door and wanted me to walk in the hallway. He was absolutely amazed and wanted to video my walking with his phone. When we returned the room, he put his hand to his forehead perplexed.

He excitedly exclaimed, "You have to understand, when a person presents with what you had, where you had it, the successful outcome of this kind of surgery is that you are either a paraplegic or a quadriplegic."

# POWER OVER THE STORMS

*He calms the storm, So that its waves are still. Then they are glad because they are quiet; so He guides them to their desired haven (Psalm 107:29–30).*

There was only one being that could have that kind of control: God Himself.

In the medical record, Dr. Shafizadeh wrote: "There was significant blood loss ... Some muscle mass of psoas muscle was removed with the cancer mass."

He said, "I have seen the muscle where the cancer was with my own eyes. You should not be walking." He went on to say that he believed that this had to be God who did this; there is no other explanation.

# GRATEFUL

*Oh, that men would give thanks to the Lord for His goodness, And for His wonderful works to the children of men! Let them exalt Him also in the assembly of the people, and praise Him in the company of the elders (Psalm 107:31–32).*

Only God could have done the work inside of me. I live because He wants me to live, and I will go to be with Him when what He wants me to accomplish is done. One day, I hope to say something similar to what Paul said to Timothy:

*For I am already being poured out as a drink offering, and the time of my departure is at hand. I have fought the good fight, I have finished the race, I have kept the faith. Finally, there is laid up for me the crown of righteousness, which the Lord, the righteous Judge, will give to me on that Day, and not to me only but also to all who have loved His appearing (2 Timothy 4:6–8).*

# STRENGTH THROUGH THE STORMS

But not yet...

In Matthew 14:22-33, the disciples are out in the middle of the sea rowing against the wind and another storm. One, I might add, that was brought on by the Lord. This time, Jesus was not with them. In the middle of the night, Jesus walked near the boat intending to walk past them. When they saw Him, they cried out, "It's a ghost!"

Jesus told them not to fear and that it was Him walking on the sea. Peter asked Jesus if he could walk out on the stormy sea with Him and then got out of the boat and walked to Jesus! We all know the story. Peter began to sink when he took his eyes off of Jesus. I think he gets a bad rap here. Who of the other guys had enough faith to get out of the boat on to the sea?

There are only two people who ever walked on water in the Bible—Peter and Jesus.

# ONCE PETER SANK, HE CRIED OUT FOR JESUS, WHO SAVES HIM.

In this story and in the story with Peter, Jesus said something similar: "Why are you fearful, O you of little faith?" and in chapter 14, "O you of little faith, why did you doubt?" In this first, I think Jesus is rebuking them. They should have trusted Him. In the second, I get the impression that Jesus is not rebuking Peter, but like a coach, He is encouraging, "Peter, you were doing great! You almost had it! It was awesome! Hold on a little longer next time."

*Jesus would say that to us as well.*

The closer we get to Jesus, the bigger the storms get. But also, the stronger our faith gets. At first, we may be hiding in the boat, scared of the storm, crying out for Jesus. But as we grow, we look to Jesus, and, crawling out of the boat, we walk to Him on the water.

That is were I want to be. That is intimacy. Walking with Jesus is walking with Jesus, whatever the surface under our feet and storm raging above.

# 2.
# TO LIVE IS CHRIST
## CHAINS IN CHRIST

B ut I want you to know, brethren, that the things which happened to me have actually turned out for the furtherance of the gospel, so that it has become evident to the whole palace guard, and to all the rest, that my chains are in Christ; and most of the brethren in the Lord, having become confident by my chains, are much more bold to speak the word without fear." (Philippians 1:12–14, NKJV)

## A PRISONER OF CHRIST, NOT OF ROME

*To recap:*

After the first surgery at the University of Texas Southwestern Medical Clinic, everything was supposed to go well. But after only a few months, I began to have pain, fevers and other symptoms. After some tests, it was determined that I had Stage 4 metastatic RCC in my spine, muscles and nerves.

After three major surgeries I was not supposed to live, let alone be able to walk. I was told by my Neurosurgeon that the best outcome for the surgery I endured was that I would be alive, but as a paraplegic or quadriplegic. It was a grueling time. Amazingly enough, I am able to walk today. I am able to breath. I am able to live.

I have spoken to many cancer patients who say the same thing as Paul. He was going through such a terrible time. At first, he was under house arrest in Caesarea Maritima, then in a rental house in Rome. But now, he had been moved to a prison close to the seat of power, the elite Roman Special Forces, known as the praetorian, Barack's. The accommodations were not as nice as in Jerusalem.

Paul would probably say that he was glad that he went through struggles, trials and difficulties. Not because he enjoyed, but because he needed them. They made all the difference in his own growth as a believer and in the lives of others who watched him go through it trusting Christ. This is also what a cancer patient goes through. I always thought my wife and I would grow old together. But cancer arrived. It taught me to live daily. Jesus said, "Therefore do not be anxious about tomorrow, for tomorrow will be anxious for itself. Sufficient for the day is its own trouble." (Matthew 6:34, ESV) Obviously this does not mean that we should not prepare for the future, but I now have a different perspective. I must cherish the daily. I must learn to love the moment, for a cancer patient realizes his own death could be imminent.

Cancer, to those who use it well, becomes a gift. I wouldn't wish it, but I also would not change it. The Lord knows what I needed.

For Paul, his suffering turned out for the furtherance of the gospel. The Praetorians knew that there were no other charges against Paul except that he preached the gospel. Since many of the Philippians were ex-soldiers and probably many of them were ex-Praetorian, they knew exactly what was happening in Paul's life.

Getting cancer, it goes without saying, is no fault of the cancer patient. It just happens, well, sometimes. There are the obvious things that cause cancer: smoking, drinking, risky sexual encounters and the like. But many cancers are not the fault of the patient. Sin is sin. Some sins result in external consequence, ie: you get drunk, expect a headache the next morning. Others can be linked to nothing. There are sins which have no outward consequences, at least for a long period of time. I remember when I was first diagnosed, an acquaintance of one of my sons told him that I must have been in some horrendous sin that caused me to get cancer! It was painful to me and my son. If cancer was the result of my sin, then what was the result of this kids unloving and judgmental attitude? Shouldn't he be riddled with a horrible disease? Sin can have consequences as I said before, but I never smoked or drank heavily or had risky sexual encounters, but I am definitely a sinner. However, for Paul, his trial was absolutely of no fault of his own except his intentional preaching of the gospel. He was suffering and taking it well because it would bring glory to God. That is the goal I want for the difficulties I have gone through. Not that I am anything or anyone special, but that if I can walk hand in hand with Christ in this, then anyone can. You can.

In his suffering, Paul didn't sit around feeling sorry for himself, but he continued the work that he was called to do. Paul was chained to different guards in day and night shifts. As visitors would come and see Paul, he would preach the gospel to them. By osmosis, the guards would begin to hear what Paul was sharing. It made perfect sense! Many of them came to Christ as a result. I could imagine at the beginning of a shift, the guard would be cold and hard. Then, by the end, would be joyful and happy. The next guard would look at the other puzzled. By the ned of his shift, he would hear the gospel, becomes a believer and be changed as well.

As a cancer patient or someone going through an extremely difficult situation, the enemy is always complacency. At least that has been my experience. It is much easier to sit in my room and watch documentaries than to go out and engage people.

Depression can set in and then on top of the already overwhelming difficulty, fatigue upon fatigue overwhelms. It becomes impossible to do anything. We must fight this by doing what God has called us to do.

The definition of the word "furtherance" (Philippians 1:12) in the ancient Greek is, "with a blow," how a hammer beats on metal. A metaphor of this is a nautical term that means, "To make headway in spite of blows." So, blow by blow, we are still moving forward, never going backward because of the trial we endure as we walk hand in hand with Jesus.

# REJOICING IN THE GOSPEL PREACHED

*"Some indeed preach Christ from envy and rivalry, but others from good will. The latter do it out of love, knowing that I am put here for the defense of the gospel. The former proclaim Christ out of selfish ambition, not sincerely but thinking to afflict me in my imprisonment. What then? Only that in every way, whether in pretense or in truth, Christ is*

*proclaimed, and in that I rejoice. Yes, and I will rejoice,"*
*(Philippians 1:15–18, ESV)*

When people realized that Paul's suffering was not of his own making (well, technically it was because he didn't HAVE to preach the gospel, but it was because he was serving Christ), they became bold to preach the same gospel. Some preached out of envy and strife. This never made sense to me. Why would you preach the gospel out of envy and strife, in selfish ambition without sincerity? Paul says that they were doing so to add to his chains.

One illustration I heard that kind of makes sense came from a pastor named Joe Focht: It's like the man who goes down to the bar in anger because his wife just told him the gospel. He is angry and starts to say, "My wife is constantly telling me about this Jesus who can forgive my sins and change my life if I would just let him. He can walk with me in all my difficulties and get me through them." The guy next to him may have just lost a child, hears this, cries out and comes to Christ.

But there are those who preached in sincerity. They heard about Paul's example to continue to preach the gospel no matter what, emboldening them to do the same, even if the circumstances could be dangerous. Paul rejoices in either way the gospel gets out, as long as it gets out there.

It is so encouraging to travel a well worn path. We know that someone has gone this way before and that there is hope that we will not get lost. Conversely, it is difficult to be a trailblazer. Every milestone along the way is new and there is no guarantee that we will make it to the next trail marker because we are making them as we go along. I remember going to my first Relay For Life event and also the Reynolds Cancer Support House in Fort Smith. Being able to speak to cancer patients who had survived 10, 15, 20 and even 25 years with cancer, had blazed the trail and shown that, however difficult it could be, the path could be walked on and I, at least for the moment, had hope to continue on. Our hope is the Gospel. The good news is that Jesus came and died and rose again. He blazed a trail where no one had ever gone. Because he lives, we know that when this journey is over, we will have life in Christ. That is the hope that Paul had. It is what drove him. When we see the example of others and the realization that they are only special because of what God has done in them, then we realize that we also have that power in us and whether we live or die, we journey on, looking to Jesus, the author (life) and the finisher (death and everlasting life) of our lives. (Hebrews 12:2)

# LIVING IN CHRIST

Christ Magnified in Life or Death

*"for I know that through your prayers and the help of the Spirit of Jesus Christ this will turn out for my deliverance, as it is my eager expectation and hope that I will not be at all ashamed, but that with full courage now as always Christ will be honored in my body, whether by life or by death."*
*(Philippians 1:19–20, ESV)*

Paul is confident that through the prayers of the Philippians and the Spirit of Jesus Christ, he will not be ashamed. As he said before, the palace knows that he is not guilty of what he is charged with. Church history states that Paul stood before the Roman Emperor Nero and was released from his imprisonment, the emperor finding no fault against him. Paul preached the gospel to this Nero, who up to this point had been a pretty good emperor. But once he heard the gospel, he went insane, rejecting it and becoming the monster we know from history. When Paul stood before Nero later, he was convicted and executed.

I must say something here about prayer. There is nothing more important to me than people praying for me and my wife and boys. I have seen God answer in powerful ways as people prayed for me. Paul had this same confidence. Prayer is so important. It is the thing that we need the most that we do the least. I remember one time when I, as a young pastor, went up to pastor Chuck Smith at a pastors' conference in Southern California and asked him how I could pray for him. You would expect someone of his calibre, a man of God, who had taught the Bible several times through and led thousands of people to Christ, would tell me that I needed to go and find someone else to pray for. But he didn't. I was a young man, too stupid to be afraid to speak to a man like pastor Chuck about prayer. His answer was that his wife, Kay needed prayer and he would appreciate me praying for her. I placed my hand on his shoulder and prayed for him,

Kay, his family and anything else the Spirit showed me to pray. At the end, this busy man graciously told me that he appreciated so much that I would pray for him. That taught me something. No matter how big I think I am or no matter how "spiritual" I think I am, I was never to reject prayer. To this day I have not, and will not. I am not ashamed, with this plea, pray for me. Thank you.

But did you notice that it wasn't in the release that Paul was going to glorify God? He said that he wouldn't be ashamed, but with all boldness, as always, so now also Christ will be magnified in my body, whether by life or by death.

# CHRIST WOULD BE MAGNIFIED BY HIS LIFE OR DEATH.

This is what I had to come to grips with through my battle. At this point, I had multiple tumors in my lungs. Would it be to the glory of God if I was completely healed? Of course! But what about the opposite? What if I died? How could the Lord be glorified in that? Paul says that he was willing to suffer for Christ that he might use the suffering he endures to bring Him glory by life or by death. I feel the same way. I don't look at my death as a defeat. I am not "losing my battle with cancer." I am winning at life if I am living for others and for the glory of God. Our days are numbered; we all have a date set for our death. How we live our life—and who we live our life for—will determine success or failure.

# TO LIVE IS CHRIST, TO DIE IS GAIN

*"For to me to live is Christ, and to die is gain."*
*(Philippians 1:21, ESV)*

In Acts 12, King Herod had just put James, the brother of John, to death. Then he put Peter in prison, intending to kill him after the Passover. Normally, this would cause some serious anxiety. Peter was chained between two soldiers and guarded by four squads. He was in the inner prison, the most secure section. He was facing the death sentence and there was no way out. What's Peter doing? Sleeping. Yep. Fast asleep. So much so that when an angel comes to set him free, he actually has to strike Peter to wake him up!

Peter knew what Paul knew: For them, to live is Christ. But to die was gain, because they were going to be with Jesus. They could rejoice either way. For most, there is only a hope in this life. Therefore, when they reach what seems to be the end, they are full of stress because this world has a hold on them. But for the believer, we can rejoice that there is hope in the next world.

My friend, Mark Fry, pastor of Calvary Chapel of Arkansas City, Kansas (pronounced R-Kansas City he used to always tell me this, me being a pastor in Arkansas (R-Ken-Saw) at the time.), was a great example. When the end came, he rejoiced to see it. He knew his days were numbered and instead of stressing and worrying, he rejoiced that soon he would see Jesus and be with his wife, who had gone to heaven many years earlier. He saw a future and a hope, even praying with someone to dedicate her life to Christ just days before he went to be with Jesus.

"You will keep him in perfect peace, whose mind is stayed on You, because he trusts in You" (Isaiah 26:3).

It is so true. When we set our minds above, we experience a peace that passes understanding. "For me, to live is Christ," Paul boldly declared. If we can say that, we will experience the peace that comes with it. But if we say anything else--"For me, to live is work" or "For me, to live is my car" or "For me, to live is making a million dollars!"—then we cannot say, "To die is gain."

# TO BE WITH CHRIST IS BETTER

*"If I am to live in the flesh, that means fruitful labor for me. Yet which I shall choose I cannot tell. I am hard pressed between the two. My desire is to depart and be with Christ, for that is far better." (Philippians 1:22–23, ESV)*

What does it mean, "To live is Christ?" Paul defines it a bit in these verses. He is longing for the Philippians and is longing for Christ. It is as if he is in a tug-of-war. It is a hard decision because he loves the Philippians so much and wants be with Christ so badly.

There were and are times in life when I have been in so much pain that I longed for Christ to meet me in life or in death. I longed to see him face-to-face. Times where streams of tears fell from my eyes like rain and I hoped shortly to feel the Savior's loving and gracious hands wiping the tears away forever and ever. Living for Christ brings a sort of yearning to see heaven now and in the future. Pain can make that wish a hunger and an ache. There are other times that living for Christ means that I want to be with my family and friends and in a pulpit preaching the gospel to people who desperately need the hope found therein. There is a dichotomy of the soul, a sort of halving of the human experience. The body aches for heaven and yearns for humanity at the same time. It is called being a Christian and knowing the Savior.

What to do? If Paul stays, he will gain more fruit for his labor. Some people have said that Paul is saying that he will be able to rejoice in the fruit he has already collected and live at ease, but this doesn't make sense to me. Paul was a man on the move. He couldn't sit still, so nothing, not even imprisonment or a death sentence, could stop him from preaching the gospel and gaining more fruit. He knew that if he were to live, he would continue to preach the word and see people come to Christ until his dying breath. For him, to live was Christ. Therefore, he would gain much more fruit by being alive.

As someone going through a life-threatening illness or other situation that is adding so much stress to your life, you must detach your thoughts away from the situation. This sounds like denial. It is not. You see, Paul couldn't change the situation. He could not choose between life or death. That was up to the emperor (and, of course, God Himself). The same is true for me. I don't have a choice. I can't wish this cancer away. But I can use the situation to be a light for Christ.

What situation are you experiencing that is boxing you in? Are you thinking that if something doesn't happen soon, you are going to be undone or that your life is over? Live for Christ. Do you want peace in the storm? Live for Christ. Do you know Jesus? If not, it is time to live for Christ so that you might say that even death is gain!

# LIVING MEANS FRUIT

*"But to remain in the flesh is more necessary on your account." (Philippians 1:24, ESV)*

To Live is More Needful for the Philippians

This almost sounds conciliatory. He reaches a high point by saying how much better it would be for him to go to Christ, but it is more needful for him to be with them.

The Philippians loved Paul and he loved them. They were like family. How do you make this choice? How do you look into your wife or children's eyes and say goodbye? Sure, to be with Christ is better, but to be with family is needful. It is hard to say so. It is hard to wait for all of us to be together again in heaven. But that is what the Christian must reconcile. We all have a disease. It is called sin and it is terminal. We need the infusion of the blood of Jesus Christ in order to counter its destructive powers. We have hope in this life and we have hope in the next. If we believe.

# REJOICING IN PAUL'S FREEDOM

*"Convinced of this, I know that I will remain and continue with you all, for your progress and joy in the faith, so that in me you may have ample cause to glory in Christ Jesus, because of my coming to you again." (Philippians 1:25–26, ESV)*

I am not sure if this means that Paul heard from the Lord that he was going to be released or if there was chatter among the praetorians that he would be set free, but he seems very confident that he would see the Philippians again. He did see the Philippians again, but later was re-arrested and beheaded by the Roman emperor Nero. By his life and by his death, Paul glorified God.

# METASTATIC SINFUL DISOBEDIENCE SYNDROME

For Paul, to live is Christ. How about for you? So many have heard the words I am about to share, and yet, they haven't taken action. We have a sin problem that has metastasized to our entire body and is slowly killing us. But there is a treatment provided by Jesus, our Savior. After living a perfect life, He was put on the cross not for His own sin, but for ours. He rose again from the dead, proving that we will rise as well. He gave us the opportunity to live for him so that we might truly experience death as gain. The question is, will you believe in Him today? Will you live for Christ, have hope in Him now, then never have to fear death? He offers that to you today.

# 3.
# DISCOURAGED
## UNDERSTANDING A FEW THINGS ABOUT DISCOURAGEMENT

---

# THE DIFFICULTY OF DISCOURAGEMENT

*"Ahab told Jezebel all that Elijah had done, and how he had killed all the prophets with the sword. Then Jezebel sent a messenger to Elijah, saying, "So may the gods do to me and more also, if I do not make your life as the life of one of them by this time tomorrow." Then he was afraid, and he arose and ran for his life and came to Beersheba, which belongs to Judah, and left his servant there. But he himself went a day's journey into the wilderness and came and sat down under a broom tree. And he asked that he might die, saying, "It is enough; now, O Lord, take away my life, for I am no better than my fathers.""* (1 Kings 19:1–4, ESV)

When I was feeling extremely low, I thought of a Bible hero named Elijah. He was a prophet. He was a miracle worker. He also fought depression. Elijah's despondency is not concealed but expressed with shocking detail in the sacred text, so when I read about him, I didn't think of myself in a different category than him. If I share the same problem, then, perhaps, I share the same solution.

# ELIJAH IS DISCOURAGED

The need for heroes is clear from ancient mythology to modern-day Marvel movies. Our culture is screaming for someone to save them and they flock to movie theaters across the country and indeed, the world, to watch their exploits. These fictional heroes allow us to, for a moment, escape the problems we face. The scriptures give us real heroes: David fighting Goliath; Daniel in the lion's den and Jonah having a whale of a time. Of these, my favorite is Elijah. He did phenomenal things like calling fire from heaven twice to consume an army standing against him, raised a widow's son from the dead and defeated the priest's of Baal, Jezebel's own regiment, who were deceiving the people into worshipping idols instead of the LORD. For this, he faced opposition from Jezebel and her feeble husband, Ahab, king of Israel.

I learned a long time ago that if I am constantly talking about how horrible my life is, how I am experiencing a bad job, terrible relationships, a terrible church, I can do a disservice to the God I love and to those who look up to me as an example. If I believe that God is good and that He is able to take care of the difficulties in my life, then what reason could I have for being discouraged?

As Christians, we have to understand a few things about discouragement and how to make sure we overcome those dark thoughts that enter our minds and attempt to destroy us. Scripture is so important. Paul told us of the treasure that a Christian possesses in Ephesians.

"Blessed be the God and Father of our Lord Jesus Christ, who has blessed us in Christ with every spiritual blessing in the heavenly places, even as he chose us in him before the foundation of the world, that we should be holy and blameless before him. In love he predestined us for adoption to himself as sons through Jesus Christ, according to the purpose of his will, to the praise of his glorious grace, with which he has blessed us in the Beloved. In him we have redemption through his blood, the forgiveness of our trespasses, according to the riches of his grace," (Ephesians 1:3–7, ESV)

From this passage, the Christian is:

1. Blessed with every spiritual blessing
2. Chosen before the foundation of the world
3. Holy and blameless in Christ
4. An adopted child of God
5. A reflection to give glory to God
6. In God's will
7. Accepted in the beloved
8. Redeemed and forgiven through His blood

This scripture gives us eight reasons why Christians do not have to be discouraged, but the honest truth is that sometimes we do get discouraged. The manner in which respond to these feelings can be instrumental in beating it.

Elijah had called for a drought throughout the land. It was devastating. But after the victory against the priests, Elijah told Ahab that rain was on its way. Ahab hurried home to tell his wife about the executions and the rain. I get the impression that perhaps Ahab was excited about what he saw. But Jezebel was not amused. She sent a message to Elijah that he would soon be dead like her priests—if she had anything to do with it. Hearing this, Elijah ran for his life into the desert, and sat under a broom tree. Doesn't that just sound depressing? It sounds like "doom tree." It is a juniper tree, really more like a large bush. It provides very little shade, but in the desert, it's better than nothing.

I remember many times being where Elijah was. Under a broom being swept over by discouragement. Cancer, my Jezebel, sent a message of doom and gloom. God had brought me through such horrible surgeries and recovery and yet, there I was, attempting with everything within me to get some relief (shade) and getting little and allowing my soul to become more and more disquieted within me. The second I heard a bad report or imaging showed something that wasn't good, Jezebel was there with her message—you are going to die! I was running from her and from everyone else, hiding away in my room.

It was at this time I was still stiff by the metal in my back and could not wipe when using the restroom. There were tools available, but they never quite worked. I was in a lot of pain, my confidence was very low, I had to allow my wife to wipe me. It was completely humiliating, but was part of my story and led me close to despair.

# HE PRAYED THAT HE MIGHT DIE.

As of the writing of this book, the NIH statistics on Anxiety Disorder is as follows: An estimated 19.1% of U.S. adults had an anxiety disorder in the past year. Past year prevalence of any anxiety disorder was higher for females (23.4%) than for males (14.3%). An estimated 31.1% of U.S. adults experience an anxiety disorder at some time in their lives.

Number of suicide deaths is 48,344 and the number of deaths per 100,000 population is 14.8. (1)

Elijah was discouraged and depressed. It is estimated by the National Institute of Mental Health [†](NIMH) that 17.3 million adults in the United States had at least one major depressive episode in 2017 (latest numbers as of print). That's 7.1 percent of the population! (2)

According to the World Health Organization (WHO), 264 million people worldwide suffer from depression. It is a leading cause of disability. I am sure the statistics are similar—or worse—now. (3)

# SIGNS AND SYMPTOMS OF DEPRESSION

If you have been experiencing some of the following signs and symptoms most of the day, nearly every day, for at least two weeks, you may be suffering from depression:

- ✳ Feeling sad or anxious often or all the time
- ✳ Not wanting to do activities that used to be fun
- ✳ Feeling irritable, easily frustrated, or restless

* Having trouble falling asleep or staying asleep
* Waking up too early or sleeping too much
* Eating more or less than usual or having no appetite
* Experiencing aches, pains, headaches, or stomach problems that do not improve with treatment
* Having trouble concentrating, remembering details, or making decisions
* Feeling tired, even after sleeping well
* Feeling guilty, worthless, or helpless
* Thinking about suicide or hurting yourself (4)

Elijah was very likely clinically depressed. He was even suicidal at times and prayed that God would kill him. This prayer does show us that, although Elijah wanted to die, he wasn't going to commit suicide.

Suicide for the believer doesn't allow God to work in your life and in the lives of others through you. But suicide for the non-believer opens up a whole host of other issues, the most important being a lack of redemption. That person will be separated from God for all eternity, not because they committed suicide, but because they died without knowing Christ.

According to the (1)NIH, suicide was the second leading cause of death among those 10-34 years of age in 2018, a year before cataclysmic Covid-19 government shut-downs caused wide-spread depression and a possible uptick in suicides in this age group and beyond. According the the (2)CDC, suicide is 10th overall cause of death and they estimate that 47,173 people died by their own hands in 2018. The (3)Who says, "Close to 800,000 people die due to suicide every year, which is one person every 40 seconds." (5)

I am not an expert in any of these fields, so if you or someone you know is experiencing any of these issues, you should immediately seek the help of a trained Christian counselor or a psychiatrist.

# JONAH IS SUICIDAL

The prophet Jonah experienced something similar to Elijah. He wanted to see the destruction of a city, Nineveh, but God had mercy on its residents instead. Jonah became bitter sitting in the heat of the day, by himself, in the wilderness waiting for God's judgment that never came. God created a plant to give him some shade, but then prepared a worm to eat and destroy the plant. That was it. Jonah couldn't handle things anymore. He loved that plant. How could God destroy it?

"And it happened, when the sun arose, that God prepared a vehement east wind; and the sun beat on Jonah's head, so that he grew faint. Then he wished death for himself, and said, "It is better for me to die than to live." Then God said to Jonah, "Is it right for you to be angry about the plant?" And he said, "It is right for me to be angry, even to death!" But the Lord said, "You have had pity on the plant for which you have not labored, nor made it grow, which came up in a night and perished in a night. And should I not pity Nineveh, that great city, in which are more than one hundred and twenty thousand persons who cannot discern between their right hand and their left—and much livestock?" (Jonah 4:8–11).

Elijah's problem was the opposite of Jonah's. He wanted national renewal and revival. He wanted it to start with Ahab and Jezebel. Perhaps, he thought, she could see from the palace that a storm was arising and that God was having mercy upon Israel again! She would now repent of all her evil and the nation would repent. But these hopes were ill conceived. He didn't understand that people are rarely convinced by evidence; they often ignore the evidence and do not believe.

It was not Jezebel's threat that put him into a depression. He had just executed 450 prophets of Baal and watched the Lord do miracle after miracle. Although the people up on Mt. Carmel said, "The Lord, He is God ..." then, in their emotion carried out what Elijah had commanded—to execute the prophets of Baal—the enthusiasm was short lived. The message from Jezebel reminded him that no matter what God did through him, the people were not going to turn back to God again.

This is one of the most disappointing and depressing things a person in ministry can ever encounter. Am I effective? Is the pain worth it? Do the people really want Jesus? Then you watch them one by one start to fall away. When Elijah says that he is no better than his fathers, he means that his effectiveness has been about the same.

Have you ever felt this way? Have you ever been so completely overwhelmed that you wanted to give up? I have. I remember when I first entered physical rehabilitation hospital, I felt hopelessness and darkness all around me. I was crying uncontrollably. The doctor came into the room and kneeled down at my bedside and held my hand.

He said, "Steve, you can't give up." I told him that I had already given up. He asked about my kids and my wife and told me that I had to hold on because of them. They needed me. I told him that I was a Christian and a pastor and I wasn't supposed to feel this way. Then I wept some more. He asked if I believed in God. I said yes. He said, "Well, God believes in you. You can't give up." I was a mess and pathetic, but God had mercy upon me.

# A PHYSICAL PROBLEM?

It had been an emotional time for Elijah. He had great highs and deep lows. He desperately needed help, so the LORD sends him an angel. When he was doing well, God sent ravens to feed him. Now, in the depths of depression, God sends an angel. The Angel makes a cake. What kind? Angel food cake, what else?

One of the causes of depression can be diet or lack of food. God, knowing that Elijah is not eating and is losing strength and beginning to feel hopeless, sends an angel cook.

Is this "an angel" or "THE Angel"? It makes a difference. If this is "The Angel," Elijah would still have much to live for. He would be used by God still. Isn't it interesting that the one who asked to die, would be one of the few in the Bible to never die? He would anoint kings and give his office to Elisha, the prophet who would do the most miracles of any in the Bible, except Jesus Himself! Then Elijah would be taken up in a fiery chariot into heaven to never die. Later, in the days of Jesus, Elijah would meet this Angel again (Luke 9:28-30), in human flesh, when he and Moses met with Jesus just before Jesus' transfiguration.

If this was The Angel of the Lord, a Christophany (Jesus in the Old Testament), then this reminds me of when Jesus appeared to the Apostles on the shores of the Galilee in John 21. He had already cooked fish and some bread. Sometimes, just eating a better diet can help to overcome depression. One of the first things I did was change my diet and juiced and ate a cancer friendly diet that was low in sugar and high in protein. I was absolutely miserable, losing a lot of weight and beginning to feel worse by the day. I remember being at a doctor's appointment just before my first surgery in Dallas, Texas. I was telling the doctor how much I really wanted a Red Robin burger with all the fixings. He said, "We have a Red Robin here. Go get one." I asked if I could eat that as a cancer patient. He said, "You are losing a lot of weight and not feeling good. Go get some food you like so you'll actually eat it." It was completely freeing and Monica and I went to Red Robin later that evening. I felt so much better and stronger and ready to fight this cancer battle.

Did the Angel mean that the journey ahead was too much for him, or was he referring to the journey he was already on? It could have been both. "You have to eat, Elijah. The journey, your life right now, is too much for you." But after eating those two meals, whatever kind of bread that was, Elijah had enough strength to travel forty days and nights to the mountain of God. The NIMH recommends treatment first, but some things to help with sadness or a depressive mood is to eat right and exercise. Elijah has a great meal and then walks for 40 days and nights, getting a lot of exercise.

But that doesn't always help. You need something more. The experts recommend having someone to discuss your problems with. Not someone who will judge you, but someone who will allow you to vent.

# THE CAVE

The "Word" of the Lord came to him and "He" said to him... In John 1:14a, Jesus is called the Word that became flesh and dwelt among us. Was this, again, Jesus?

I definitely believe so.

> *Jesus says, "What are you doing here, Elijah?"*
> *(1 Kings 19:9; ESV)*

The question is interesting. How was it said? Was it in a bad tone? Accusatory? Was it kind? Was it neutral? Where was the inflection? "What are YOU doing here?" or "What are you doing HERE?" I like how God opens up the dialog. Jewish scholars believe that this cave was the one where God put Moses when He was going to reveal his "afterglow" in Exodus 33:22. This is not "a cave," but "THE cave." Perhaps God was telling him to look at where he ended up, which is right here in His presence and to think about why he was there. He is allowing Elijah to speak freely. Elijah's response tells what his problem was. He was self-consumed.

"I have done everything right and still nothing has changed! I am the only one who serves you!" (My interpretation). But it was good for Elijah to express this. We'll see in a moment God's reason for asking the question. Stop and read Job 2:11-13.

# RESPONSES TO DISCOURAGEMENT
## A CORRECT RESPONSE

The first—and correct—way to respond to a person who is depressed or going through an enormous amount of difficulty in their lives is to sit with him and be kind. Paul wrote to the Romans telling them to rejoice with those who rejoice, and weep with those who weep (Romans 12:15).

I was hurting both mentally and physically. Meds were clouding my mind as bad as the PTSD was strangling my heart. I needed to get the pain I was feeling on the inside out to anyone who would listen. I was expressing what was in my heart. Some of the things I said were probably not that scriptural, but I appreciated those that would listen. I didn't need them to say something about God being good in a time when I was feeling like He had crushed me. I know that wasn't the truth now, but in that state, it felt as though they were telling me to shut up and take it. I know it sounds strange, but I just needed *to see* the goodness of God working through people rather than hear them say how good He was. From the many hurting people of whom I have spoken to, they feel or felt the same way. There will always be time later to correct someone's doctrine, but now, they just needed love in a tangible way—like I did.

Some people in church have a tendency to give quick answers to deeply hurting people because they don't want to have to deal with the hard work of helping them to dig out of their problems. We have become a soundbite, social media-based society where everything we say has to be in compartmentalized 280-character spurts that may be inspirational for the moment but are never lasting.

Job is another hero of mine. I know, that sounds strange. How could the man whose very name equals painful trials be of any kind of hero. Although he had his problems, his friends were almost worse. Job thought he could trust his friends to just listen; they thought that Job needed commentary on everything he said, even accusing him of being in sin because he didn't trust God. But in the end, Job's friends were the ones rebuked by God. How did Job get out of his depression? The same way Elijah did: God revealed Himself to Job. He had a lot of questions and believed that if he were to ever stand before God, he would be able to demand accountability. In Job's mind, God was on trial and therefore, He must answer for criminal conduct that God had committed. But in the end, it was Job that was on trial. God never answered the questions, but He did show Himself to Job. When Job saw the glory of God, the realization of His awesome mercy set in. Job no longer needed God to answer. He had all the answers he needed just by being in His presence. So many people say that when they get to heaven they will ask God why He did this or that. I don't think that will be the case. I think we'll all be like Job—speechless. When we see the goodness of God we find the light in the darkness and a peace that passes understanding. That is why it is important for us to model Jesus in someone's life. The only thing that brings someone out of emotional downfall is the revelation of Jesus Christ—an experience with God.

# OVERCOMING DISCOURAGEMENT
## A STILL SMALL VOICE

The LORD passed by, just like He did with Moses. But God was not in the tornado, the earthquake or the fire. Funny, these are normally called "Acts of God." Elijah is told to go out and stand on the mountain before the Lord and expect God to move. This would have been an awesome sight to see. But Elijah almost seems apathetic toward it all, however, a still, small voice—a whisper—gets his attention in 1 Kings 19.

# A SUCCESSFUL MINISTRY

Was this the voice that told him to go out and stand on the mountain? Perhaps. Elijah was obedient and went to hear more from the Lord. When a person is depressed, he wants to isolate himself. God asks the question again. What are you doing HERE, Elijah? Look around, does this place look familiar? What do people who usually come here want? They want to see God's glory, right? Is that why you are here Elijah?

Then Elijah repeats what he said earlier. I like God's answer: "Go." God's answer is for Elijah to continue to do what he was doing. His work was not in vain, and there was much to live for. God would be magnified and His will done.

# HERE ARE SOME PRACTICAL WAYS FROM THE SCRIPTURES TO OVERCOME SADNESS:

**Laughter.** "A joyful heart is good medicine, but a crushed spirit dries up the bones." (Proverbs 17:22, ESV). Monica and I determined two things regarding this. The first was that we would never go to bed sad. So, we decided to find a funny sitcom or some other show online or on DVD that would make us laugh. It did us good indeed! And two, that we would always attempt to make my oncologist laugh by the end of the visit. The reason? He sees death every day. He has to tell someone they are not going to make it. He is there when they are in the hospital when they are about to die. We wanted him to experience some joy, if even just for a few moments while Steve and Monica were there.

**Friendship.** "A friend loves at all times, and a brother is born for adversity." (Proverbs 17:17, ESV). Without our friends and those who were and are still praying for and supporting us, we would never have made it. They are more valuable than they will ever know!

**Don't isolate yourself.** "Whoever isolates himself seeks his own desire; he breaks out against all sound judgment." (Proverbs 18:1, ESV). This was very difficult.

When going through an intense trial, we immediately want to isolate because it is too difficult to be around others both physically and mentally. It takes work, which sometimes equals stress. But it was so important to get out. Sometimes it was important just to go to church or to the store to see other people. I found that once I was isolated, it was easier for me to stay there. The more I got out, the better I was and the easier things became. I encourage you, if you are stuck inside, to take baby steps and go outside. Get with other people who love you and will not place extra burdens on you.

# LOSING ALL HOPE

When I was in the throes of difficulty, I remember when I lost all hope and was crying all the time. The Lord had to remind me that although I was a pastor, I was also human. Somewhere along the line, we got this idea that we are not to share our stories of struggle with people. Somewhere along the line, we were told that we needed to shut people down who were struggling with depression or sadness because they just weren't trusting God. Without you being the compassionate voice of Jesus in someone's life, they will never find their way out of the darkness and into His glorious light.

Think about Jesus. In John 12, he knew that he was going to raise Lazarus from the dead. Yet He still wept for his friend and for the people around. Later, in Matthew 26:37, as Jesus was praying in the Garden of Gethsemane, Jesus was so distressed that He didn't want a Bible study or a quick Tweet, but for His closest friends to watch and pray with Him. And Paul, writing to his friends, the Corinthians, told them of his great distress in 2 Corinthians 1:8-11.

Having feelings of sadness is not wrong, but human. God created believers around us to be our support, pointing us to Himself. I hope and pray that this book, so far, has been that for you. You are loved, even though things may look hopeless now. Jesus has not left you. He is with you. Call out to Him in your trial, and you'll find that the Lord is good.

# 4.
# FOUR TESTIMONIES
## POWERFUL TESTIMONIES TO APPLY TO OUR LIVES

---

# PSALM 107

We should give the Lord, thanks because He is good and His mercy endures forever. God is good. I love that God had called me to pastor a small, southern church in Fort Smith, Arkansas. Since it was a completely different culture, I had to learn a lot. One of the things was that when I would say, "God is good!" The people would respond, "All the time." Then I would say, "All the times," and they would say, "God is good."

It was a fun reminder that He IS good. What is good? God. The Hebrew word for good is תוב, (Tov), which can have a wide range of definitions. It can mean good as opposed to bad. It can mean prosperous or blessed. It can mean that a bad situation has become good. Good is one of those things that we can all recognize but find difficult to define. Ultimately, since God is good, everything that is good should be defined by what God is. Therefore, we find good when we find God.

Jesus had an interesting conversation with a wealthy young man who was a political figure of the day. It is found in the Gospel of Luke chapter 18.

*"Now a certain ruler asked Him, saying, "Good Teacher, what shall I do to inherit eternal life?" So Jesus said to him, "Why do you call Me good? No one is good but One, that is, God" (Luke 18:18–19).*

The ruler recognized that Jesus was God because Jesus was a "good" teacher. After this quick conversation, Jesus asked the young man to leave all his riches, give them to the poor, and then follow Him. Only God could ask such a question and demand such loyalty. Jesus is good, therefore, Jesus is God. God is good. The ruler? Not so much. He ends up leaving sorrowful because he understood that he didn't have possessions, but they had him.

In Psalm 107 we see the nature of God's goodness. He is good, therefore, He does what is right, regardless of what we may perceive as right or good. He is good and His mercy (Hebrew word: חסד (chesed, merciful lovingkindness) lasts forever. His goodness and His love endure even when we would think they should not. The psalm is primarily about the goodness of God and His love on display through four testimonies. (Let the redeemed of the Lord say so.) After this, we get an idea of why God does what He does, and why we have to go through the difficulties we endure.

# TESTIMONIES
## THE WANDERER

*Psalm 107:4-9*

Have you ever felt lost? No matter what you did, you couldn't find your way. It was not necessarily through any fault of your own, circumstances happened and you found yourself wandering around. I have lived this way. I was homeless for a while when I was in college, so I know what it is like to not know where my next meal was coming from. There comes a certain point in our lives that we must realize that we are not alone. We may be running. We may be lost. But we are not alone. As the psalmist says, "They cried out to the Lord in their time of trouble." (v.6) God is only a cry away. When you cry out to Him in your trouble and distress, you find that your loneliness goes away and you realize that God was with you the whole time. He has found you. And He has answered you.

I love that it says "straight way," (v.7) and that there is a city. It kind of reminds me of when Jesus told His disciples that he had a place prepared for them (John

14:1-4) and that he would not leave them as orphans (John 14:18). in Hebrews 11, those of faith are called aliens and pilgrims because they are only traveling through, looking for a homeland in the heavens:

*"For people who speak thus make it clear that they are seeking a homeland. If they had been thinking of that land from which they had gone out, they would have had opportunity to return. But as it is, they desire a better country, that is, a heavenly one. Therefore God is not ashamed to be called their God, for he has prepared for them a city." (Hebrews 11:14–16, ESV)*

We are all looking for a place to call home. We are searching for the city of God which is a place of rest and peace. So we give thanks to the Lord because He satisfies the longing soul and fills the hungry soul with goodness (v.9). We must understand that God's goodness is not measured by what we think is good, but in the nature and character of God, in what He knows to be good. We find satisfaction where God dwells, in His city; and dwelling in that city we find His goodness. So, when trouble comes our way and we cry out to Him, we find our satisfaction in knowing the Lord and in trusting Him.

This is the first of the four testimonies. The ancients believed in similar things as we moderns. When overwhelming trouble hits us that is beyond our means to overcome to whom do we turn? We circle back to the one who is building the city of God. We pivot toward the one who has granted us citizenship in that city and we know that in Him we find peace for our situation in the now looking forward with eager anticipation to the then. We don't have to be The Wanderer anymore for we have found a place to dwell —in Christ—the city of God.

# THE PRISONER

*Psalm 107:10-16*

Those who find themselves in difficulties that are not of their own making are found in verses 4-9 and 23-32. But what about the person who has made huge mistakes? What about the man who disregarded what was good or the woman who didn't listen when they were told their lifestyle choices would have grave consequences?

You might have done something in your past for which you would be ostracized if it were made known. Perhaps you spent some time in jail. Perhaps you are headed there soon. Is God willing to help you? We often write off people like this as "beyond salvation." But God never does. Perhaps you have created a prison of your own through your addictions or desires. Has God abandoned you? No. Are you so depressed that you are about to commit suicide? Have you fallen and feel unable get up? David went through this very thing. He said in Psalm 40:

*I waited patiently for the Lord; and He inclined to me, and heard my cry. He also brought me up out of a horrible pit, out of the miry clay, and set my feet upon a rock, and established my steps. He has put a new song in my mouth —Praise to our God; many will see it and fear, and will trust in the Lord (Psalm 40:1–3).*

Instead of taking matters into your own hands, cry out to God. You are in darkness, in the shadow of death. There is no question. There is no delay. Even people who have scorned the counsel of the Lord can find forgiveness and hope in Jesus. You can be delivered out of your distress. He takes away the chains. He releases you from prison and sets you free.

What ails you today? What do you need to be set free from? Whether gates of bronze or bars of iron are holding you, God cuts you free! Cry out to God and He will set you free!

This is the second of the four testimonies. We are no longer The Prisoner if we trust in the LORD. There is true, unquantified and unshackled freedom in Jesus, in fact, that was His mission:

*"The Spirit of the Lord is upon me, because he has anointed me to proclaim good news to the poor. He has sent me to proclaim liberty to the captives and recovering of sight to the blind, to set at liberty those who are oppressed, to proclaim the year of the Lord's favor." (Luke 4:18–19, ESV)*

*Psalm 107:17-22*

# "SIN IS AT THE BOTTOM OF ALL SORROW, BUT SOME SORROWS ARE THE IMMEDIATE RESULTS OF WICKEDNESS"

-CH Spurgeon, Treasury of David

# THE AFFLICTED

The word here for "fool" in the original Hebrew means, wait for it, fool. This is someone who knows what is right and does the opposite. He despises counsel. Consider Proverbs 12:1, my middle son Jared's favorite verse. It says:

*"Whoever loves discipline loves knowledge, but he who hates reproof is stupid." (Proverbs 12:1, ESV)*

It is his favorite verse because it has the word, "stupid" in it. This describes the fool in Psalm 107:17. The fool does stupid things but doesn't realize nor think about the consequences of his actions. The affliction here is some sort of illness.

It is true that we live in a fallen world and that all sickness and death are a result of sin. But our disorder may not be a result of our specific sin. Just because we are afflicted, doesn't mean we are in sin. My battle was not just physical dealing with aches and pains. It was spiritual. With every new ache I felt, I would think that the cancer was back with a vengeance and that

God was condemning me for my sinful attitude or fleshliness or because I was grumpy and argued with my wife. The only thing that helped was the knowledge that God had already cleansed me of my sin upon the cross and that I was free from condemnation. Of course those who desire to love and serve God with all our hearts, want to be obedient, but when we are not, we have the advocate, Jesus Christ, the righteous.

"This testimony is speaking about a person who, being told that getting drunk and partying all night long will get you sick the next day, does it anyway. Or, he is one who is told that sexual sin can give you a disease that can kill you and then commits the sin anyway. This is a person who lives a constant lifestyle of thumbing his nose at God's grace and therefore is reaping the consequences of his actions. Paul said so much in Romans 1 regarding a Christ-rejecting world that would rather follow the dictates of their own consciences than the Word of God. Into all that we might expect God to say that He has had enough of these people and that they should all just spend eternity in hell. It is amazing to me how quick I am to judge others. When I do, I find that I am the farthest from the kind of compassion consistent with the heart of God.

Moses, in Numbers 20:10-13, did this once and lost the blessing of entering the promised land because of it. God wasn't mad at Israel, but He wanted them to trust Him. God does not write people off, He redeems them and He rescues them. He heals them! When they get to the point where they just can't handle the consequences of their sin anymore they finally cry out to God.

# LOOK HOW HE HEALS THEM:

They cried out and He saved them out of their distresses. How? He sent His Word and healed them and delivered them from their destructions. (v.20) How is that? He showed them where salvation could be found. He showed them wisdom and understanding. He showed them their Messiah. Jesus is the Word of God (John 1). Jesus brings healing. He is the balm of Gilead (Jeremiah 8:22) He died on the cross in the greatest display of love this world has ever seen. The

Word of God points to Christ. Jesus told the religious leaders of His day:

*"You search the Scriptures, for in them you think you have eternal life; and these are they which testify of Me"*
*(John 5:39).*

He healed them. This is our God! He doesn't throw anyone away. Therefore, those who realize their error and come to Christ will rejoice with singing! They will praise the Lord louder than any other. They needed the Great Physician, and they found Him. Remember, it is the sick who need a doctor, not those who are healthy!

This is the plight of The Afflicted, the third testimony of the four to show God's amazing grace. We are no longer The Afflicted when we look to Jesus for our healing.

# THE SAILOR

*Psalm 107:23-32*

According the New Zealand Maritime Museum's web site, the most superstitious of sailors would have, "No bananas on board. They were believed to be so unlucky they would cause the ship to be lost. Whole cargoes of bananas were especially frightening for sailors." Right in the middle of their list of 20 frightening things that sailors believed over the years is the day in which a sailor could begin a journey. "It was bad luck to sail on Thursdays (God of Storms, Thor's day) or Fridays (the day Jesus was executed), the first Monday in April (the day Cain killed Abel), the second Monday in August (the day Sodom and Gomorrah were destroyed), and 31 December (the day on which Judas Iscariot hanged himself). There are all sorts of things that will set a sailor on edge. From bananas to the day the sailors would split (jk), there can be nothing nothing scarier than going out to sea.

Like verses 4-9, those in verses 23-32 come to trouble just in the normal course of business. They aren't doing anything wrong. They aren't doing anything out of the ordinary. Then, BOOM, they are hit with the storm of storms. Notice that it is "HE" who raised the stormy wind. Their soul melts because of the trouble. "they reeled and staggered like drunken men and were at their wits' end." (v.27)

One thing after another hits these sailors. Wind. Waves. Swells. Fear. And then finally they get to the point where they lose all hope. Monica and I experienced a "sailor" moment when a retina doctor told her she would need emergency surgery for a torn retina in three places and had already lost part of her vision. We just looked at each other and laughed. It wasn't the response the doctor was used to getting. We told him that "She may go blind, I have stage four kidney cancer. I have had multiple surgeries, and she is going to have surgery. You call it disaster, we call it Thursday."

*"Then they cried to the Lord in their trouble, and he delivered them from their distress." (v.28)*

*There is no question. God delivers: "He made the storm be still, and the waves of the sea were hushed... and brought them to their desired haven." (v.29-30)*

This reminds me of when the disciples were in the boat with Jesus in Luke 8. These were seasoned, professional fishermen who had spent their lives in boats. They did not scare easily.

A storm arises. Jesus is asleep ... perfect! Does it seem to you that every time you need God, He's asleep? It is not because He can't deliver you or doesn't want to. It is because He is teaching you to trust Him. The disciples found this out when they awoke Him and said, "Master, don't you care that we are perishing?" Of course He cared. He asked them, "Where is your faith?" It was as if Jesus said, "I trusted you enough to leave you alone in the storm, couldn't you trust Me that I didn't leave and that I have this all under control even when it doesn't seem like it?" He had earlier told them that they were going to the other side. They should have trusted Him.

We are always going to be delivered, but along the way, it may get rough. This is the evidence of the redeemed who went out to sea. They came back and avowed in the assembly of the people, and praised God in the company of the elders. This is what happens for someone who is like The Sailor, the final of the four testimonies. They go from trial to struggle and difficulty through storm and in the end, they tell whomever will listen that God is Tov and Tov is God.

These accounts are extremely important. If we do not share our report, how will people know about the goodness of God?

What happens when things don't go the way we planned? What if the boat had sunk? What if the sickness would have killed the fool? What if the prison door would never have been opened or the wanderer never found a home?

The testimony is not in the deliverance, but in the goodness of God. God is good regardless of our situation. You see, the testimony shows contentment. They were delivered because they were content in God. The same is true for us regardless of our situation or its outcome.

# THE REASON FOR DIFFICULTY

*Psalm 107:33-38*

## RESTORATION OF THE LAND FOR THE POOR

Do you understand what God does? He turns rivers into wilderness, water springs into dry ground, a fruitful land into barrenness. God does these things. They don't seem to be in line with the testimonies in the previous verses. In fact, they seem to be the opposite. But God is in control, and He has reasons for doing what He does. It is those places of difficulty and trial where He calls the hungry to dwell. There they find a city for their dwelling. He changes things for those who need to know the goodness of God.

Paul said it this way in 2 Corinthians 1:

*Now if we are afflicted, it is for your consolation and salvation, which is effective for enduring the same sufferings which we also suffer. Or if we are comforted, it is*

*for your consolation and salvation. And our hope for you is
steadfast, because we know that as you are partakers of
the sufferings, so also you will partake of the consolation
(2 Corinthians 1:6–7).*

As I speak at churches I sometimes get feedback
on how the message went. Some people are very
gracious and say that they were thankful that I spoke
at their church. Others tell me that they were moved
by the message. Others, though, I can see in their eyes
that they can relate to what they just heard. They have
pain in their faces and agony in their eyes. They are in
pain not only for themselves, but for loved ones or
friends that they love. They speak from the heart. One
such person told me that he was shocked that I was
out speaking because I am going through the very
things that I am speaking about. Most people will tell
their testimony after they had gone through
something, but from their perspective, someone going
through it, is an amazing testimony of the goodness
and grace of God. If it was my sin that made me get
cancer, then praise God that I am a sinner! But I don't
think it was. I think I was one of these four and all of
them at the same time. I was the Wanderer, the
prisoner, the afflicted and the sailor all wrapped up into

one package. I needed to be saved. Salvation to the ancients was not a one time thing, but a process. This means that I am being saved, not from sin, that was taken care of at the cross, no indeed, I am being saved from my daily life. I am being saved from the old man, from the cares of this world and, yes, from the prison of my illness. In that is the goodness of God. He is my salvation and my song; my joy in whom I trust! So my difficulties only serve to show others the goodness of God and I am more than okay with that. It makes my life worth something and my experience have meaning.

# CONTRAST BETWEEN THE LOFTY AND THE LOW

*Psalm 107:39-42*

There is a difference between those who humble themselves before the Lord and those who are full of pride. If you are willing to surrender to God, He is willing to bring you to a place of peace. Call out to God as the storm arises and realize that you are not alone.

He is with you and will never leave you, even though at times in life he will seem as though he is asleep. He is not. He is surely awake and watching you stand firm on his promises. Stand firm and stand sure. You will find your place of rest in the arms of our God and Savior Jesus Christ.

# UNDERSTANDING THE LOVE OF GOD

*Psalm 107:43*

The psalmist wants us to understand these things. Observe them. Find out about them. Is God good? Then follow Him. You can have that peace. Cry out to Him out of your dark place. Cry out to Him if your rebellion has brought nothing but a prison cell. Cry out to Him if you are afflicted and need wisdom. Cry out to Him if your storm is overwhelming!

# 5.
# MY LIFE IS HIS
## NEVER GIVING UP

---

*Acts 20:13-24*

# "WHEN CHRIST CALLS A MAN, HE BIDS HIM COME AND DIE."

– Dietrich Bonhoeffer, The Cost of Discipleship

*"Every athlete exercises self-control in all things. They do it to receive a perishable wreath, but we an imperishable." —*
*The Apostle Paul, 1 Corinthians 9:25*

Sometimes we have to wonder if what we are doing is worth doing. We have to weigh the options and make sure we are walking on the path where we've been called. I like wildlife documentaries. We see the finished product on the screen and are enamored by the story of a family of lions or a leopard mother trying to survive with her cubs. What we do not see is what it took to get that footage—the countless hours in the bush, fighting the bugs, the malaria, the animals themselves! All are dangerous. All can be the cause of their deaths. But, for some reason, the producers have counted the cost and believe what they are doing is worth it. One particular couple, Derek Jobert, a wildlife videographer and documentarian, and his wife, Beverly, a wildlife photographer, almost paid the ultimate price when a bull cape buffalo gored Beverly and knocked Derek to the ground. They both survived, but it was close.

In Luke 14:25-33, Jesus told His disciples that discipleship has a cost. They would be required to pick up their crosses and follow Him. They would have to count the cost and see if they had what it would take to complete the "project" on which they were working. The Gospel must be first and foremost. To them, it was more important than life itself. They counted the cost and considered loving Jesus and loving people worth giving their life. This is calling. The animal documentarians work for a crown that perishes. We do it for an everlasting crown, because we love Jesus and we love of people. It is important for us to understand that in life, there will always be difficulties and trials. Some will go through things that on the outside seem more difficult than others. But to them, it is their "stage4" of life. I was diagnosed with stage 4 cancer, others were diagnosed with stage4 bankruptcy, others with the stage4 loss of their dream job. If I am not prepared for these tragedies I will not be able to survive them when they come my way.

The best way I can prepare is getting to know my Lord and Savior more and more each and every day.

# SOME TIME TO BE ALONE

In the scriptures we see the apostles, the disciples, the church and even Jesus praying. Communication with God is one of the best ways we can gain peace in a situation that is overwhelming. Some prayers are flippant, oh, not meaning to be, but nonetheless, are. They are the, "bless this food," or "thank you for this day," type of prayer that whether we said them or not, would not change much in our lives. Then there are those times when we have to get away from everyone else and every distraction for a time to talk to God.

Yes. Prayer is really just communicating with God. It is telling him our troubles and difficulties. Not that he doesn't know them, but so that we have someone to express them too. Believe me, I needed this type of prayer many times through my battle. I felt alone many times even though I had my wife with me. There were even times when she could not come to my aid. But God? Yes. I could go before him and know that he would listen. Tragedy brings this out. There are groans and moans that only God can interpret and know the answer to apply.

# JESUS' EXAMPLE

Jesus loved people and wanted to teach them and tell them the good news about himself and the Kingdom of God. He loved to see them healed and even to answer their questions. But there were those times that he needed to get away and spend some time alone with his Father.

*"Immediately he made the disciples get into the boat and go before him to the other side, while he dismissed the crowds. And after he had dismissed the crowds, he went*

*up on the mountain by himself to pray. When evening came, he was there alone," (Matthew 14:22–23, ESV)*

*"But now even more the report about him went abroad, and great crowds gathered to hear him and to be healed of their infirmities. But he would withdraw to desolate places and pray." (Luke 5:15–16, ESV)*

He is our ultimate example. He was very God of God on earth. He was powerful and lived a life like none other. And yet, even he needed to spend time alone in prayer. If he is our example, then shouldn't we spend a similar amount of time in prayer? Of course the answer to this question is yes.

I thought a lot about prayer. Especially as a small church pastor before I was diagnosed with cancer. For three years before the diagnoses, I spent every day in at least two hours or more of prayer. I wrote my prayers down at the time in a digital journal and, due to a hard-drive crash, all of them were deleted. Perhaps God wanted those cries and praises just for himself. I didn't see them as fruitful, I thought of them as necessary at the time, but couldn't see the results. On the de-commissioned side of the Fort Chaffee Military base, there was an amphitheater that, at the time, was overgrown and unused but afforded a great view of the city of Fort Smith. At my dining room table me and member of our Fellowship spoke passionately about prayer and decided that we, along with some other select brothers, would meet at the amphitheater once a week to pray for the city and for the churches and pastors in the area. We could literally see the buildings of about 80% of the city from our vantage point. Both my prayers and meeting together lasted about three years and a little longer for the other guys while I was in the hospital and recovery for six months.

I believe these times of prayer were instrumental in my ability to get through some of the most difficult times in my life. A devotion to prayer is what got me from point B to point A. Obviously those precious times of prayer yielded more fruit than I could ever imagine as I was upheld in the toughest battle in my life. So, yes, I went from spending time by myself, then spending time with others in the presence of Jesus. This is a good order. Sometimes we need to be alone with God. Other times we need our brothers and sisters in Christ to stand in the gap for us. While I was recovering it was once again time for me to pray on my own. My prayers became more personal. They weren't flippant. They were serious business with God; impassioned cries before my Father who loved me and would listen to me even when my whimpering didn't make much sense. He still loved me and I could pour out my heart. The need to be alone and the need to be with others is important. Being with others encourages us.

*"And let us consider how to stir up one another to love and good works, not neglecting to meet together, as is the habit of some, but encouraging one another, and all the more as you see the Day drawing near." (Hebrews 10:24–25, ESV)*

When I did finally get home, I needed my brothers and sisters once again to come around me and to pray for me. As I wrote in an earlier chapter, it was difficult at times as I stared at the four walls or drowned myself in animal documentaries. I got so used to being alone that it was unhealthy because I was just alone, not seeking the Lord, just alone. That is why I needed people to pray for me with passion.

*"Therefore, confess your sins to one another and pray for one another, that you may be healed. The prayer of a righteous person has great power as it is working." (James 5:16, ESV)*

When I was focused on prayer both with others and alone with God, I was able to tackle any challenge that came my way. But I noticed a sharp difference when I wasn't praying. I became weary and worn-out. I was once again fearful and couldn't handle the stress. But once I realized the problem, I would devote myself to prayer again and fear would cease. Prayer is a powerful tool. It puts is right into the presence of God where we find hope, joy and peace. There is nothing like this on earth.

## THE WITNESS OF THE HOLY SPIRIT

Like Bonhoeffer said,

# "WHEN CHRIST CALLS A MAN, HE BIDS HIM COME AND DIE."

We have to understand what calling is and how it relates to our suffering in life. I learned early on that I could go through anything, any kind of difficulty or trial or suffering as long as I knew that God was with me. That is why prayer is so important. When we pray we see the greatness of God and this helps us to understand how small our problems are. When we pray, we should also pray for big things and have to understand that the most impossible thing we could ever think about asking does not even come close to the power of God to accomplish it. Nothing is too difficult for him. Our suffering is also bearable when we are close to the Father. He consoles and comforts us in our difficulties. Is suffering part of the plan? What about difficulty and trial? Will it happen to us if we are walking closely with Jesus? Truth is, the closer we are to Jesus, the more of a target we get on our backs:

*"Indeed, all who desire to live a godly life in Christ Jesus will be persecuted..." (2 Timothy 3:12, ESV)*

Paul also told the Philippians:

*"For it has been granted to you that for the sake of Christ you should not only believe in him but also suffer for his sake..." (Philippians 1:29, ESV)*

The road will be difficult. If I am committed to the plan of God in my life and how it can effect the lives of others through the gospel of Jesus Christ, I must answer that I am willing to take that road on my journey. Again, the choice is not made in the storm but way before the storm, back when I first came to Christ. It is the only way to survive when the winds and waves hit. This kind of strength does not come from me. I would shrivel up and die in my own power. I am only strong because of what Christ has done for me and that he has left me the greatest of all gifts, the Holy Spirit to work in and to make me more like Jesus, who was willing to suffer and die. It was shameful what they did to him, but it was necessary to save us from our sin. It was necessary so that we could have the Spirit of God living inside of us, changing us. This is whom I rely upon. I am his to do with as he sees fit, suffering or abounding in goodness, I am his. Even in difficulty, he has never steered me wrong. I have always known him to be good.

# GOSPEL OF GRACE WORTH IT

The Gospel of grace is worth much more than my life. I am insignificant on the grand scheme of things. My life is a blip on the radar. But for the sake of seeing someone come to Christ, I want to be a big bold and bright blip! In order to do this I must be determined to surrender myself in such a way that God's plans are worth my suffering.

I do have to make a bit of a determination here that may change a bit of semantics, but not much else. My suffering was through cancer a disease that is the result of the fall where sin entered the world through our first parents, Adam and Eve. The suffering that the early Christians went through in the scriptures was a choice they made. They knew there would be persecution because they decided to preach Jesus. But they did it any way. They knew that they would more than likely end up in prison for their stand. If prison was where their next ministry was going to be, then that was where God wanted them.

My suffering was not a choice I made *to* suffer, but a choice *in* suffering. If I would have been given the choice to not go through cancer, then at the time I would have asked to be relieved of it. I would have missed so much opportunity to give others the gospel and the growth that God did in me, but before I knew that, I would have said, "No way!" I didn't get that choice, and praise God, he is taking me through it and making me more like him daily.

But that is where the semantics end. I still have to make the choice daily to get up and to face the day no matter what may come. I have to make that choice in following Christ or my own flesh. These choices come only from begging the Holy Spirit to fill and give the strength that I need to do even the most mundane of things. I love that he makes valid my invalidities. He still uses this broken down body for his glory. It is the only way I get through what I do.

God has given me his mission. It is my calling. You'll read about this in a later chapter, but the verse God gave me as my marching orders was:

*"But I do not account my life of any value nor as precious to myself, if only I may finish my course and the ministry that I received from the Lord Jesus, to testify to the gospel of the grace of God." (Acts 20:24, ESV)*

# "NEVER, NEVER, NEVER GIVE UP."
– Winston Churchill

You must be willing to give up life and limb to win the battle. My life has significance as long as I am on God's side and I only fail if God himself fails, and if that is the case, then there is nothing worth fighting for. We are in a battle that we must never give up. The enemy has taken souls captive and we must free them with the only thing that will open the prison doors, the key, the gospel of Jesus Christ.

*For I consider that the sufferings of this present time are not worthy to be compared with the glory which shall be revealed in us (Romans 8:18).*

This is what gets us to the point of being willing to suffer for the name of Jesus. We have counted the cost. We have seen that it is worth the suffering. Are the eternities and souls of men, women and children worth putting ourselves in grave danger? Is it worth losing our lives? The answer is Yes. The call of God tells us there will be bumpy roads and pain, but also the triumph of seeing people come to know the Savior. That's worth it to me. I would rather be preaching the gospel in pain than sitting in the lap of luxury in complacency.

# 6.
# THE LORD IS MY SHEPHERD
## A JOURNEY OF A LIFETIME

---

*Psalm 23*
*The Lord is my shepherd; I shall not want.*

## "WE HAVE ALL THINGS AND ABOUND; NOT BECAUSE I HAVE A GOOD STORE OF MONEY IN THE BANK, NOT BECAUSE I HAVE SKILL AND WIT WITH WHICH TO WIN MY BREAD, BUT BECAUSE THE LORD IS MY SHEPHERD."

– Charles Spurgeon

Psalm 23 is probably one of the most quoted chapters in the entire Bible. It is quoted at funerals and at the bedsides of those who are going through the darkest of times. This psalm has brought comfort as many tried to find meaning in their difficulties. The psalm describes a journey. It is the story of a Shepherd who leads his flock from green pastures, through the valley of the shadow of death and to the house of the Lord forever. I encourage you to stop reading this book and pick up a Bible and read Psalm 23. You will get far more from those six verses than this entire chapter, but if you want my experience, after reading that chapter, finish reading this one.

Psalm 23, more than anything else, helped me through the difficult times that I experienced after my surgeries. I quoted and wept through these verses, realizing that the LORD is my Shepherd and that I did not have to fear. C.H. Spurgeon once wrote:

"Suppose an accident should take our lives? I smile as I think the worst thing that could happen would be the best thing that could happen. If we should die, we shall be with the Lord (1 Thessalonians 4:17). So, if the worst that can befall is the best that could come, why should we fear? This is good reasoning. If you are a believer, and God is your refuge, there is no logical reason why you should ever fear."

I have learned that God is my refuge and a very present help in my time of need. He is with me and I can take shelter, literally, in his name. Psalm 23 opens with the name of God. Our translation renders (יהוה) as "The Lord," and in Jewish translations it is either Adonai (the Lord) or Hashem (the name). The name is where I take my shelter because it expresses who God is. He is known and unknown at the same time. His name is mysterious. We understand just the surface of the surface of the nature of God. If God were an ocean, we'd still be in the parking lot, paying the meter for parking in our knowledge of the almighty. His name is so great that I can get lost in him.

When I was struggling with life and death, I needed to know that God was all powerful. I needed to have a God that I didn't completely understand, but at same time was full of grace and compassion. There is no help for me from a dispassionate unmerciful higher power. If God is not personal, then I am lost in his unknown benevolence or indifference. That is why reading Psalm 23 affected me so greatly. When the shepherd-king David wrote this psalm, he was either young and tending sheep, or old and remembering back to his days when he was out in the wilderness with his flock. I like to think that he was old and remembering back because he needed to know through all his difficulties that God was going to be his personal shepherd like his sheep were to him.

# THE LORD IS MY SHEPHERD.

I don't own God, but he is my own God. The Shepherd is my shepherd and I am his little lamb. I was in pain with disease. Sheep do get diseased from time to time and the shepherd has to be a shephysician sometimes. God was mine. He was with me. I knew that he carried me. I knew that he was there, guiding me, comforting me, having compassion on his pitiful, miserable sheep. His personal touch and loving presence carried me when I never thought I would ever get through. He is personal and he is with me and he is my shepherd, leading me to where I could experience rest and healing.

The psalm continues in its medicinal flow; "The LORD is my shepherd, I shall not want." Sometimes there is a mis-understanding here. It is not that I shouldn't want, or that I will get everything I want. A better way to understand this is that we won't be in want of any good thing, or we will get everything that we need. This is the responsibility of a shepherd. He is duty-bound to take care of his sheep and to make sure that they get the food, water, medicine and protection that they need. Sheep must feel confident that their shepherd is taking care of them or they will get nervous and eventually get sick and perhaps even die. When I am trusting that God is my shepherd and that he will provide for every need that I have, I am at rest in the midst of the most difficult time. He is my peace because, the little I know about Him, is more than I ever need to know about his ability to satisfy my soul and my belly, when I am in need. Through every financial struggle, of which there have been many (cancer doesn't just ravage your body, but eats everything else as well), God has taken us through and we have survived. Resting. Trusting. Knowing. Provision. These all tell me that there is a Shepherd in heaven that loves me and that will lead me on this journey called life.

# THE JOURNEY

*Psalm 23:2*
*"He makes me lie down in green pastures. He leads me*
*beside still waters." (Psalm 23:2, ESV)*

Speaking of journeys, shepherd-king, David describes a journey from the plush, pristine pasturelands of the Shepherd's fields during the spring and summer, toward the grazing grounds where the sheep will be safe throughout the winter. When summer draws near again, the journey moves back to the house of the Shepherd, the place of green fields and still streams.

In the summer months, sheep are content in green fields and still waters. In order to rest, sheep must lay down, but they are fearful creatures and will not lay down unless they are made to do so. My heart was as broken as my body. Tears were flowing at any turn of events in the early days, so I was always stressed and was never able to rest. My wife has been wonderful through it all but that doesn't mean she has always been nice. Sometimes nice was not what I needed, but a swift kick in the pants, figuratively speaking. I really believe that the Holy Spirit used Monica to tell me that I had to lay down and had to get some rest. Once I did, I was able to sense the moving of the Spirit, speaking to me and saying that I would be well taken care of and that I could rest without worry. When the Spirit of God moved this way I migrated from my bedroom to a green pasture with a quiet stream where I could see my Shepherd and know that I was okay, until the next time I felt the stress. It was a battle, but as much as I relied upon the LORD, he sustained me in it all. This was only at the beginning of the battle, I would find out. It got worse as time went on.

# RESTORATION OF MY SOUL

*Psalm 23:3*
*"He restores my soul. He leads me in paths of righteousness for his name's sake." (Psalm 23:3, ESV)*

Winter makes food scarce, so the sheep must be led to a place where they can graze during the cold season. It is at this time the sheep must stay closest to their shepherd. Being on the right path is important, ensuring they will arrive at the place where they can be cared for. When I was in the deepest, darkest place as I went through surgery after surgery, the only thing that could comfort me was to know that God was with me, leading me, and restoring my soul. Usually we think that when trials and difficulties come, we are on the wrong path. In response, many will veer off the path and try to find comfort. But that doesn't lead us to the place where God wants us to be. Part of the journey is that winter will come. It has been said that you are always in the middle of, entering or at the end of a strenuous time. There are only hints of peace in the midst of life's difficulties and the way to get through life is to learn how to have peace in the midst of the burden than to try to get out of it. In Psalm 23, the paths mentioned in verse 3 are well worn. We have to remember that we are with the Shepherd even though we are experiencing a punishing and demanding life. He hasn't left, in fact, he is the one leading on this well-worn path, which means we are on the right path.

# THE SHADOW OF DEATH

*Psalm 23:4*
*"Even though I walk through the valley of the shadow of death, I will fear no evil, for you are with me; your rod and your staff, they comfort me." (Psalm 23:4, ESV)*

There is actually a path that is jagged and steep in Israel called the Shadow of Death (Wadi Qelt, or "The Way of Blood") where Jesus walked into Jerusalem on His way to the cross). It begins in a valley, then wraps its way through the cliffs, then upward toward the winter grazing grounds. It was a very difficult journey, but it had to be taken. Jesus would eventually take the path and die on a cross for us. If our Savior took an onerous and brutal path in saving us, then we can be assured that going through something light in comparison (our struggles) is also the right path.

Shepherds lead from the front, the sheep must follow close behind. If they take their eyes off the shepherd, they could die. We also must keep our eyes on our Shepherd, Jesus, during this journey. One thing I understood, as I was going through my life with cancer, was that I was experiencing the "shadow of death," not death itself. It was a preview of death, but God was there, leading and guiding every step of the way. I have to tell you that when the cancer was in my body, and even a few months after the surgeries, I could feel death inside of me. In fact, I didn't want to make any long-term plans because I didn't know how long I would live. I used to look at Ezekiel, Daniel and the book of Revelation as travel brochures. These books describe heaven and I thought that I would be there some time soon and wanted to know more about where I would be traveling! When I remembered that God was with me, I began sensing life in me again.

# ROD AND STAFF

Rods and staffs were instruments a shepherd would use to bring wayward sheep back in line. Similarly, God uses trials and difficulties as His rods and staffs to do the same for us. For some, a little nudge does the job; for others, hard blows. Some of us need to get smacked. Some of us need to be grabbed around the neck by the crook in the shepherd's staff. Whatever way, the trials and the difficulties should be a comfort to us because it means that we are getting ever closer to God.

# A TABLE AND ANOINTING

*Psalm 23:5*
*"You prepare a table before me in the presence of my enemies; you anoint my head with oil; my cup overflows."*
*(Psalm 23:5, ESV)*

In his book, *The Lord Is My Shepherd, Robert J. Morgan tells a story he read from Allan C. Emery, an advisor to Billy Graham. When he was a young man, Allan experienced something that made a lasting impression. Allan stayed with a shepherd overnight in Texas with a shepherd who had 2,000 sheep. As it became dark in the field, just as the sheep were calming down for the night, he could hear the yelps of coyotes in the distance. The shepherd began to put a couple more logs on the fire. At once, Allan could see what looked like thousands of little lights in the field, then he realized it was the fire reflecting off the eyes of the sheep. Instinctively, the sheep did not look into the darkness or toward the coyotes, nor did they run away, but placed their eyes on the shepherd. (1)

Two of Robert J. Morgan's books fit into my story. The LORD is my Shepherd, and The Red Sea Rules. They both gave me comfort in a dark time when I really wasn't sure how life was going to go. I needed to know that God hadn't forsaken me and that he was still with me through all the darkness and difficulty. I would highly recommend both of them for anyone going through a time of stress. I devoured these books and have since read them several times.

I was that poor little lamb, wondering why winter had come and unable to see in the darkness except the light from the fire of God's presence. My eyes must have been glowing as I stared into the flame, searching for the eyes of the Chief Shepherd, Jesus. He delivered me in preparing a table. I learned that if sheep are nervous, they won't eat. I guess that is like a lot of us as well. They won't eat until they are at peace, and once they are, they eat no matter what is around them.

I was the same. After going through massive surgeries and now recovering, I felt alone and in need of some sort of encouragement. I barely ate. Like I have previously written, I was crying a lot. But once I began to see the light I started sensing a peace come over me. It did not overwhelm me at first. It wasn't an all or nothing thing. It was little by little. There was fear. Then there was fear/peace, then there was peace/fear, then there was peace and some fear. I wish I could say that I always have absolute peace, but I don't think we get there until we are in the presence of our Savior. Even to this day, as I am writing, I am thinking about a few times when I had scares. A questionable report or some unexplained pain or heart palpitations. I get nervous and then I must remind myself, "What is the worse that can happen?" I could die. "Ok, so I get to go to heaven!" I say out loud! Then I am okay, until the next time I have to have this conversation with myself.

I have learned to have peace in the presence of my enemies. The greatest enemy of humanity is death. But God has overcome that by sending his Son, Jesus, to die for us and to raise again so that we can live forever with him. No wonder a lamb could be at peace when his Shepherd prepared the table. There was no need to worry because the power of the enemy, which has always been and always will be, fear of death, has been overcome. Therefore, I am at peace. But something I spoke about earlier is what happens next.

The shepherd would also anoint his sheep's skin with oil to refresh them. An overflowing cup means that they have more than enough. They are safe and thoroughly refreshed, even in a time of difficulty. We should know that our God refreshes and strengthens us on our journey. He promised in John 14 not to leave us as orphans, but that he would give us the Holy Spirit. The oil represents the power and refreshing from the Holy Spirit in our lives. Without that power, I could not have continued. The Spirit of God was the practical and tangible presence of God inside of me giving me the sense of peace that I needed so desperately. Every book and every conversation can only go so far. They lead me toward God, but there is only one person that can take the journey a step further. He is the one who lives inside of me developing me, changing me, pointing me to Jesus in each and every situation. Perhaps you thought that I would say something other than the Holy Spirit for practicality and tangibility. But there is nothing more tangible than his work inside. That is the secret power of the journey. The oil keeps me going, letting my eyes see the Shepherd and letting me know that I have not lost my way and I can trust that I am on the right path, going in the right direction. My cup truly does run over!

# THE JOURNEY ENDS
## INTRODUCTION TO VERSE SIX

*Psalm 23:6*
*"Surely goodness and mercy shall follow me all the days of
my life, and I shall dwell in the house of the Lord forever."*
*(Psalm 23:6, ESV)*

This Shepherd's psalm is so important because it
gives a 10,000 foot view of the leading and guiding of
the Good Shepherd on this journey through life and in
the course of time, to the house of the LORD forever.
From green fields to the paths of righteousness
through the valley of the shadow of death eventually
leading to the table where eating in his presence is full
of peace. Like all journeys, this one must also come to
an end. We don't know when the end will come, but
we know it will come. We also know what it will be like
as well. Explore it with me in this next section.

## GOODNESS AND MERCY

I am not sure if David had sheepdogs. Every
shepherd in modern times has them. If David had

them, their names where probably "Goodness" and "Mercy." The function of the sheepdog was to protect the sheep. If any of the sheep take their eyes off the shepherd and begin to walk a different path, the sheepdogs would bark and snip at them to get them back in line. They don't do this out of a disdain or even because they want to hurt the sheep. No, they love the sheep and are willing to give their lives for them. Sheepdogs have been known to work in tandem. One dog goes after an attacking wolf; the other gets the sheep to safety. Our spiritual sheepdogs, Goodness and Mercy keep us in line. It is God's goodness that sometimes snips and barks at us and keeps us on the path. Mercy leads us back to the path when we've gone astray.

In Hebrew, mercy is the word, חסד (Chesed). It means an unconditional, loyal or steadfast love, and it is the equivalent to the Greek, αγαπε (agape). God's goodness and mercy transform us into people of the path that will eventually lead us to the home of the Shepherd where there are pastures so green and water so still that the thought of them can barely come into our finite minds.

The journey began with trusting Christ as my Savior and the realization that he was and would be my Shepherd. The journey takes faith. I must trust the Shepherd to lead even though the road is sometimes rough. The day I surrendered my heart to Christ, I knew where I would end up. On every grave marker there is a beginning date and an end date. In the middle there is either space or a dash. Cancer, surgeries, pain, medicines, depression all reside in that space. Just because you are assured of a destination doesn't always mean it will be smooth sailing all the way there. Following the Shepherd gets us there. Once we are there we get to enjoy the beauty of the house and the fellowship of the Shepherd forever and ever.

The psalm is talking about heaven here. It is the ultimate destination. Everyone wants to go to heaven but nobody wants to die! I didn't want to die and I still don't have a death wish. I want to continue to be a dad to my boys and to stay with my wife. I want to continue to tell people about Jesus and what he has done for me. I know that when the time comes, I will have mixed emotions. But I will be secure in knowing that I did not lose my battle with cancer. That is an impossibility. I won because I will be in heaven with Jesus. I look forward to that day and the eventual reunion with my family after they enjoy long and fruitful lives of their own.

I will live my life as if my days are numbered. In Psalm 90:12 the writer wants us to number our days to gain a heart of wisdom. That means that we are all finite. No one dies before their time and no one lasts longer, we all have a date with destiny. What we must do is live our lives to the glory of God. That is what I want to do. Will I always live up to that cal? No. But it is within my heart to wake up each morning wondering what God will do with the day that he has given me. I begin the day searching his word for marching orders or encouragement. The next step is to go out and do whatever he puts in my heart to do. Cancer does not limit me. I must live like a man who is dying and a man who will never die. Listen to his voice as he removes fear and provides for every need:

*"The good shepherd gives His life for the sheep. But a hireling, he who is not the shepherd, one who does not own the sheep, sees the wolf coming and leaves the sheep and flees; and the wolf catches the sheep and scatters*

*them. The hireling flees because he is a hireling and does not care about the sheep. I am the good shepherd; and I know My sheep, and am known by My own. As the Father knows Me, even so I know the Father; and I lay down My life for the sheep" (John 10:11–15).*

So, this is our journey: We begin in the green pastures, trusting our Shepherd until winter arrives. The Lord wants to take care of us through those times, so He leads us to another, more suitable, field. He prepares us along the way. We are being prepared for the difficult times in life. We walk the righteous path in His name, and we learn to trust him as we walk through the valley of the shadow of death. As we continue to follow, we get to that field, even though the enemy surrounds us.

No matter what happens to us here, we will dwell in the house of the Lord forever. We will return to those green pastures and still waters—that is heaven. There is so much to look forward to on this journey! So, it is all about Jesus, our Chief Shepherd.

It is about trusting Him in this life and for the next. No matter what happens, we know that He is with us, and we can trust that He will always take care of us.

# 7.
# THAT I MIGHT KNOW HIM
## GIVING MY LIFE TO CHRIST

## "TO TRULY KNOW GOD WE MUST LONG FOR HIM WITHOUT ANY OTHER MOTIVE THAN REACHING GOD HIMSELF."
-A.W. Tozer

When I speak at churches and get a chance to talk to others, I am asked what scriptures help me as I traverse this cancer battle. Some scriptures were for the beginning like Isaiah 41:10, which taught me not to fear, others don't always makes sense, so I think they might be just for me, or for a future time. Then there are those that transcend time. In my journey to know God in the midst of the storm, Paul's transparency in Philippians 3 was just what I needed.

> *"that I may know him and the power of his resurrection, and may share his sufferings, becoming like him in his death, that by any means possible I may attain the resurrection from the dead. Not that I have already obtained this or am already perfect, but I press on to make it my own, because Christ Jesus has made me his own. Brothers, I do not consider that I have made it my own. But one thing I do: forgetting what lies behind and straining forward to what lies ahead, I press on toward the goal for the prize of the upward call of God in Christ Jesus."*
> *Philippians 3:10–14, ESV*

This makes sense for me on so many levels. The suffering that Paul went through was because of his stance that Jesus was the Christ which so many of his fellow religious leaders did not agree. He not only suffered ostracization at the hands of those former friends, but they brought him before riotous crowds which beat him and put him in prison. His pain was because he was a believer. My pain was because I got cancer AS a believer. Yes, there is a difference. Paul had a choice, but in his suffering, he wanted to know Christ and I want the same thing. I have a choice as well. I can choose to follow Jesus or I can choose to fall back and deny him because of my pain. When I look at Paul's example I choose what he chose. I want to know Jesus and the power that comes to all who understand the implications of a dead man being alive. If Jesus is alive, then that gives me great hope. There is so much in these verses that mean so much to me.

# STRENGTH TO ENDURE IS FOUND IN KNOWING CHRIST.

*"that I may know him and the power of his resurrection, and may share his sufferings, becoming like him in his death, that by any means possible I may attain the resurrection from the dead." (Philippians 3:10–11, ESV)*

Knowing Christ is the most important thing in my life. It is an ongoing experience. When someone asks if I know Christ, my response should be, yes, and no. Of course I have been introduced to Christ. Over the years, I have gotten to know a lot about him through his word and his grace poured in me through his actions of love and mercy. Daily I get to know him as he speaks to me both in prayer and in my daily reading. But to say that I KNOW him, would be stretching it a bit. God is, by his very nature, both unknowable and knowable. We can get to know him, but we will never completely understand him. But each and every day, I fight to know him just a little more than I did before.

Strength to endure is found in knowing Christ. He has suffered so much, and in doing so, allows me to get a glimpse into his character. A God that is willing to suffer to show love invites us into his presence that we might intimately know him through his trial and the eventual overcoming of the greatest enemy we could ever fight, death itself. I felt very alone while fighting through my pain. I fought and am fighting cancer. You may be going through another painful experience. Either way, in our trouble, we feel alone. When we meet someone who has gone through a similar experience or even something more difficult that our own, we feel a sort of kinship. Those on the outside will never understand, but you and I will. We become family and we instantly find camaraderie.

That is what it means to know Christ in suffering. He is family. He knows our suffering and we know his. His suffering comes with a hope that one day he will put an end to every difficulty and trial and wipe away every tear from our eyes. That is resurrection power. If he rose from the dead, then we will also rise. We have confidence in this great power to overcome the impossible and give us the strength to live today with a future and a hope.

# JESUS HAS MADE ME HIS OWN.

*"Not that I have already obtained this or am already perfect, but I press on to make it my own, because Christ Jesus has made me his own." (Philippians 3:12, ESV)*

Jesus has made me his own. Those words alone bring such comfort. I am not alone, I am his own. There is a fight that every person who has a chronic illness must endure. Those with a terminal illness know that it is only in Christ can they find peace and healing. But that does not mean the fight ends. It can not endure, but we must press on in our own fight. I had to learn this lesson while in Physical Therapy. I started in a wheelchair, then was able to walk a few steps, then finally, I was able to walk out of the hospital on my own two feet.

The first day I was there, I remember feeling sorry for myself. I was ready to give up. I had Stage4 cancer and had just gone through major trauma both physically and emotionally. As I have said, I was weeping an awful lot. My heart was broken and my spirit was not far behind. My Physical Therapist (PT) came into my room early in the morning, it was a Saturday, which meant group therapy. I told my PT I didn't want to go. He would have none of it and forced me to get out of bed and into my wheelchair.

As I entered the large room, a semi-circle of people which bandages on their heads, necks, arms, some in wheelchairs, like me, others, seated in chairs. Our first exercise was to throw a large ball to each other in the circle. Some of the people couldn't raise their hands very high, others had a hard time thinking. Some were getting angry at their inability to do the exercise and began yelling and screaming. I listened to some of their stories. One young man was drunk and early one day that week had missed his turn and wrapped his car around a telephone pole. He would never walk again. Another had brain surgery. They would never be able to think clearly. Another young man was injured in a Football game and, despite everything they did medically, it was possible he would never play the game he loved again. Each was experiencing a horrible loss. A thought came to mind, "Jesus would be among these people." Then I realized, he WAS among these people.

I would rise up, walk and leave this hospital. Many of these would never have that opportunity. I had to fight and press on even if things looked bleak, at the very least, I would walk again and be able to do many things on my own. That was my goal. And as I pressed on, I would tell as many people as I could about the God who was with me, and the God I was getting to know more and more through this terrible fight.

# I DECIDED TO BUILD MY HOUSE ON A ROCK.

*"Brothers, I do not consider that I have made it my own. But one thing I do: forgetting what lies behind and straining forward to what lies ahead, I press on toward the goal for the prize of the upward call of God in Christ Jesus."*
*(Philippians 3:13–14, ESV)*

I am not finished. I will never be finished until the day that Jesus calls me home. The longer I live, the more I realize how much I have to learn. I get to know God by allowing him to use my inadequacies, trials and difficulties for his glory and to encourage those who are going through something similar. The struggle is current. I am going through the fight, having good days and bad days. But I know that the things I go through have a purpose. They work together to assist me in knowing God, and that gives me the strength to continue to serve him even in the most trying of circumstances.

People often ask me two questions when they hear me tell my story. The first is, How did you get through everything you went through, and the second is, How are you doing it now? Believe it or not, they are questions I have asked myself. How could I have gone through three major surgeries—a total of 23 hours—in only 11 days. During the longest surgery, the doctor implemented metal rods and screws in my back to support my spine after the cancer had eaten through two of my vertebrae, a quarter of the way in surgery, a friend thought that he would read on Facebook any time that I had gone to be with the Lord. How is it possible that 7 years later I am holding the line with metastatic RCC, had my lower lobe of my right lung removed and now diagnosed with a secondary bladder cancer and I am still smiling? How can I speak at churches, write devotionals, minister to people who are dying, and in the process of writing this book? Shouldn't I be laying in bed waiting for the last breath? No. Why? Because I made a choice long ago that profoundly changed who I was going to be and how I would be able to survive anything sent my way. What was that choice? I wish I could tell you that it was a choice to be a good person or to even have a good attitude. I wish I could tell you it was because I knew the Bible so well and cold rattle off scripture by scripture in memory, but it wasn't any of these things, although they are all good things.

Years ago, when I was 16, I decided that I would fight cancer some day and endure it, even though I had no idea I would be diagnosed with cancer. I know this sounds strange, but I made the choice that would give me the strength to fight anything that came my way. I decided to build my house on a rock.

In Matthew 7, Jesus tells a story about two men who were building a home. One of them started with a foundation of rock. The other decided to build on the sand. They both had nice houses that looked good on the outside and were good and functional on the inside. Then, out of nowhere, a storm arose and wind and rain began to beat against the two houses. The man who built on sand had to run away in fear and lost everything because the storm ripped his home apart. I have been to many storm ravaged places as part of a team doing relief work. We were in Joplin, Missouri after an F-5+ tornado destroyed a large portion of the town. We were in Bay St. Louis, Mississippi after super storm Katrina destroyed communities from Mississippi to Louisiana. I went with "Extreme Makeover, The Home Edition" to New Orleans to rebuild a church and a home ruined by Katrina. But the one place that stuck out to me was when a tornado went through a small town in Arkansas called, Mena. As we drove around looking for opportunities to serve people, we noticed something strange. Homes were completely destroyed on one side of the street, and were barely touched on the other. I am not sure the reason that the tornado missed one side of the block and destroyed the other, but I do know why the man who built his house on the rock's house was saved. He built it on a firm foundation. In the story, Jesus says that his Word, trusting in the Gospel, is the firm foundation.

In giving my heart to Christ, I built my house, my life, on a firm foundation. When rain and flood came, ie., cancer and the ensuing surgeries, months of physical therapy, being diagnosed with metastatic cancer again and again, pill form chemo and all the side-effects, immunotherapy and having a horribly painful reaction, the worse pain I have ever been in due to metastatic cancer in the pelvic area, radiation and finally being diagnosed with a secondary bladder cancer, I felt the winds and the pouring rain, I felt the flood of tears! And yet, in all of this, my decision rang true, my hope secure, my life was built on a rock and I will never fail because of it. I will get stressed sometimes. I will cry out to God in fear at desperate moments. I am still capable of anxiety. But that does not negate the rock I am on. I may be a few 2x4s and some dry-wall when I finally see Jesus, but he will make me new, giving me a new body that will never have disease again.

# KNOWING JESUS IS NOT ABOUT INFORMATION, BUT IT INVOLVES INFORMATION.

I have hope in this world and in the next. There are medical advances and treatments that I can try. But when all these fail, I know that my faith is firmly in Christ. I do not have a death wish, but as I am writing this, I am in tears. I look forward to seeing Jesus and to experience healing like I have never known. That is my yearning and confidence. My life is in the hands of Christ. The years He gives I pray that I am able to be used to bring many souls to him and to see his people grow in their faith, hope and love. Praise God, I am alive. Praise God I will be more alive than ever when I see him face-to-face.

Some day, someone will say, "Steve lost his long battle with cancer." Oh, they are so wrong. I will not have lost my battle, I will have finally won! I have done so because of a decision made when I was sixteen years old. My life is built upon the Rock and there is no storm that can destroy it! It is essential, therefore, that I know him and the power of his resurrection that brings the strength to live or die.

Suffering has a strange way of forcing you to change your priorities. It doesn't change the nature of your character. Suffering doesn't make you a better person, necessarily, but does bring to the surface the person you are on the inside. This is why suffering can transform some people into monsters and others into saints. There are those who become people of mercy, being grateful for the life they have, rather than the life of ease by the removal of suffering. For me, I had to re-focus my pain toward Jesus. I learned and am learning how to use the hardship for Christ. It is only in using my trauma for his glory does suffering make any sense. In essence, I had to get to know Jesus all over again.

Knowing Jesus is not about information, but it involves information. I get to know Jesus by spending time with him and talking to him and listening for him to speak to me. Often in times of difficulty, we get the time to do just that because we can't really do anything else. When I was on my back in bed, there was little choice but to listen to him through his word and talk to him in prayer. It didn't stop there, it is ongoing; it is something that will last until I stand before him in heaven. It is like talking to a "pen pal" through letters and on the phone, but never really being in the same room with them. One day though, we will be in the same "room" and knowledge will be perfect.

# A WALK WITH JESUS TAKES TIME.

There is a story in the Bible that I really enjoy. The extent of the story is one verse:

*"Enoch walked with God, and he was not, for God took him." (Genesis 5:24, ESV)*

I wonder how this happened? This is pure conjecture, but I think it was like this: God and Enoch walked together every morning. They talked and got to know each other. The conversations got longer and longer. Enoch each time would look back at the house and return until he was so far away and the conversation was so good that he forgot about his life in the past and continued toward the future, which was the life with God. He got to know God so well that God took him. That is the kind of relationship I want and I know that is the relationship that Paul had with Jesus. It takes a lifetime to get there and it starts with a conversation. You never get to know anyone closer than when you suffer with them. There is a bond that becomes so close and so personal and so intimate that it is nearly unbreakable.

# THERE IS FELLOWSHIP IN SUFFERING.

*"that I may know him and the power of his resurrection, and may share his sufferings, becoming like him in his death," (Philippians 3:10, ESV)*

I am convinced that when a Christian suffers, it is counted along with the sufferings of Christ. This is not the atoning work of Jesus on the cross, obviously, but Jesus is walking in the sufferings with us. I used to think this was only referring to suffering you encountered while preaching the gospel or while standing up for your faith. But I don't think so anymore. The enemy is after all of us. He wants to take us out.

He cannot bore you to death; he cannot argue you out of the Kingdom; however, he may attempt an all-out assault. That is suffering because you are a Christian.

What are you going through today? Are you suffering on your own? The question is, do you know Jesus? Are you suffering with Jesus? Is He carrying you through, or are you doing it on your own? I was diagnosed with Stage 4 Renal Cell Carcinoma and had multiple surgeries that potentially could have taken my life. I wasn't supposed to be able to walk. To say the least, it was a difficult time. I had to learn what it meant to go through an incredible amount of pain realizing that I could not get myself through it.

I leaned on my caretaker, my wife Monica, much of the time. I knew I might not be able to think because of all the drugs and surgeries, but she had extensive medical knowledge and could watch and make sure the hospital was doing things correctly.

We went through those rough days hand in hand. She constantly gave me Scriptures and loved me with a selflessness that I have seen in precious few. We have gone through so much together; there is no way I could ever find that in anyone else nor would I ever want to. She is my love. My caretaker. My dearest, loveliest Monica. But even she could not handle the load. It was overwhelming. There was only one person that I could get to know well enough to have the power to overcome and to intimately walk with me through all that pain and that was Jesus Christ.

There is fellowship in suffering. There is intimacy. There is understanding and peace. When we suffer together, something happens and we get to know each other on a deep level.

# YOU MUST BE DEAD

The interesting thing about heaven is that every human there, with a couple of exceptions, had to experience death. Death is the part of the human experience God, up to the point of the cross, had never experienced. Of course, he is God, so he has always understood death and knew everything about it except experience.

*"In the days of his flesh, Jesus offered up prayers and supplications, with loud cries and tears, to him who was able to save him from death, and he was heard because of his reverence. Although he was a son, he learned obedience through what he suffered. And being made perfect, he became the source of eternal salvation to all who obey him, being designated by God a high priest after the order of Melchizedek." (Hebrews 5:7–10, ESV)*

He learned obedience through what he suffered. Jesus had to die in order to be resurrected. Not only that, but he learned what it meant to truly live in the context of suffering. I understand life's nuances when bits of life are taken from me. When I try to help my wife bring in the groceries or attempt to get something for her off of the top shelf, I realize that a bit of life has been taken from me. I appreciate those things much more now that they have been taken from me. I no longer take them for granted and therefore, I long for a life where these restrictions are no more.

To know that Jesus, the God-man, experienced the same thing through his sufferings, helps me to know him better. He knows me intimately and I trust him intimately. He suffered the loss of life, I suffer the loss of life daily in the little things. It is in those little (huge) things, I get to know the God that sustains.

I understand that God knows everything. I take that on faith to this day. But it helps that he is not a God who created us and then left us to fend for ourselves. He was willing to come and be one of us that we could truly get to know him. Without Jesus becoming a man, we would still be cowering in fear of the cloaked God who dwelt behind a vail of holy darkness. But now I am able to look to Jesus, who understands my pain and is willing to walk with me in it. That being the case, I can endure all things, for God is with me and will never leave, even when in the severity of my suffering.

# 8.
# A BROKEN LIFE
## STRENGTH IN WEAKNESS

F or certain people, humility is not enough. They need to see the diploma on the wall (education) or letters from the "right" people, churches, or church leaders. I understand that, to a point. But people are not defined by a certificate or letters after their name. Don't get me wrong. I love education and I consider myself somewhat educated. It helps in conversations and opens doors. But it does nothing for our status before God. The greatest scholar and the lowliest sinner all get into heaven the same way, a relationship with Jesus Christ.

If you use your education in a humble way to bring people to Christ, then it becomes a valuable asset. But if it is used to say how wonderful you are, then it becomes a millstone around your neck and people will only see you, not Jesus. We have to understand that Knowledge puffs up, but love, builds up. (1 Corinthians 8:1) Life, a good life, is about loving others and bringing glory to God. The way we do that is made clear in different ways, but it is revealed in the sincerity of a humble, grateful, broken life. The more you are used by God, the greater the struggle becomes.

# "HE ALSO BEGAN TO WEAR DOWN EMOTIONALLY, SUFFERING BOUTS OF DISCOURAGEMENT AND DEPRESSION"

*"In 1527, Martin Luther experienced a trial so severe that church historian Philip Schaff described that year simply as 'the disastrous year.' It was the time of Luther's 'severest spiritual and physical trials.' As the leading figure of the Reformation, Luther paid a high price in the struggle for truth, and his physical condition deteriorated under the movement's mounting demands. On April 22, 1527, Luther was so overcome by dizziness in the pulpit that he stopped preaching and was forced to retire. Other physical*

*problems followed for the Reformer, including severe heart*
*problems, digestive ailments, and fainting spells.*

*He also began to wear down emotionally, suffering bouts*
*of discouragement and depression" (1)*

# SPURGEON WENT THROUGH SUCH DIFFICULTIES AND STRUGGLES AND EVEN DEPRESSION.

He wrote: "I pity a dog who has to suffer what I have," and "I often wonder, to this day, how it was that my hand was kept from rending my own body in pieces through the awful agony which I felt when I discovered the greatness of my transgression." And again, "To my great sorrow, last Sunday night I was unable to preach. I had prepared a sermon upon this text, with much hope of its usefulness; for I intended it to be a supplement to the morning sermon, which was a doctrinal exposition. The evening sermon was intended to be practical, and to commend the whole subject to the attention of enquiring sinners. I came here feeling quite fit to preach, when an overpowering nervousness oppressed me, and I lost all self-control, and left the pulpit in anguish." (2)

The great apostle, Paul had a thorn; a messenger from Satan.

*"So to keep me from becoming conceited because of the surpassing greatness of the revelations, a thorn was given me in the flesh, a messenger of Satan to harass me, to keep me from becoming conceited." (2 Corinthians 12:7, ESV)*

God was doing a phenomenal job in given vision after revelation. It was abundantly clear that he was an extraordinary servant of the most high God. This clarity over time had the potential to derail the great apostle. God allowed the enemy to cause all sorts of harm. Perhaps it was an illness or frustration in ministry. Either way, Paul needed to understand that although he was being used greatly, he was still just a broken sinner, saved by grace.

I have been there. I remember being unable to stop crying one evening after I had spent five weeks in the hospital (18 days in ICU) and then transferred to a physical rehabilitation hospital. The doctor at the facility knelt down beside me and told me that I could not give up. I told him I had already given up and that I couldn't take any more. The surgeries were too much. So was the recovery, the meds, the depression I could not overcome. I was done.

But the doctor asked if I was married and had kids and if I could be strong enough for them. I told him that they would be better off without me. Then he said, "Do you believe in God?" I told him that I was a pastor and that I wasn't supposed to feel this way, but I said I did believe in God. Then he said, "Well, He believes in you!" I needed that. I needed to know that the Lord was with me and that His grace was sustaining me. I was absolutely broken.

We do not always need a memorized, catch-all scripture verse to stab people with. Becoming the verse in the lives of those to whom we are ministering is much more powerful. A verse like, "I can do all things through Christ who strengthens me," can be demonstrated by standing with someone in their pain, rather than just quoting the verse. Another verse like, "He will never leave you, nor forsake you," can be lived out, without even quoting it, by not abandoning your friend, but staying near and loving him.

Simple things like this breathed life into me as I was in that physical rehab facility. I appreciated this approach so much when people would come to visit, or a nurse would act in a compassionate way toward me. Only later did I realize their encouragement was actually scripture lived out and it became powerful. Crushed people need to be unburdened, then they can be told what the source of that unburdening was. At least that is what helped me the most. Oh, there were people who would do nothing but quote scripture at me. I know they meant well, but their words seemed aloof, something they knew, but never experienced. The most powerful scriptures were those lived before me in living color, not black and white on a page.

Remember, even God demonstrated His love by sending His Son to die for us. (Romans 5:8) He not only spoke the word, but acted it out. It is important for us to do the same.

To the broken Jesus says: "I know you are going through a lot in your life right now. You are aching and in pain. You are having a hard time. You are depressed. You are weeping! I know how you are feeling. I endured the cross. I know what it is like to suffer. I endured the mocking crowds. I endured the beating of the Roman whips. I know that it is too much for you to handle on your own. But you are not alone. My grace is sufficient for you, and in your weakness I am made strong!" (1 Corinthians 12:9)

He says that to each and every one of you today. He knows what you are going through and sometimes He wants to use your struggle, difficulty or thorn in the flesh for the glory of God. He may not take it away, but He will pour upon it the most powerful anesthetic ever created: the grace of God!

# HOPE IN WEAKNESS

We have to experience the struggle to know the grace. There is strength in weakness. There is power in the knowledge of our own mortality. I am weak and I am foolish, but He is wise and strong. Therefore, if I am successful in this life at reaching people for Christ, they will not look at how I accomplished it, but they will say, "How in the world did God use that guy?" Then, it will be, "If God used him, then God can use me or anybody!" And that is why His strength is made perfect, complete or whole in our weakness.

It is far better to boast in my inabilities than in my abilities. It is better to speak about my foolishness than about my wisdom. I am not able to accomplish anything apart from Christ. I feel it intimately that if He is not immanent, I feel lost! This is why I think Paul was struggling with some sort of disease or illness, perhaps even his eyes. Our difficulties become our special envoys declaring to us and others the power of God in our lives.

# PLEASURE IN WEAKNESS

This is what gives me hope when I am torn apart. I can almost take pleasure in the struggle because I know that my brokenness is not only changing my heart, but also being used to help others. My goal is to bring pleasure to God and to let you know that there is hope in your affliction.

"The Lord is near to the brokenhearted and saves the crushed in spirit." (Psalm 34:18, ESV)

Infirmities, reproaches, needs, persecutions and distresses. We don't take pleasure in the pain itself, that would be masochistic, but we do take pleasure in what the pain produces. The pain that we go through produces a nearness to God that can not be obtained any other way. He is close to us in our pain not just because he understands it, but because his heart breaks to see those he loves so dearly in such travail.

For me, the process of pain opened up my eyes to see God's patience and kindness. As he carried me when I couldn't walk and spoke comfort to my heart when all hope was lost, I knew that no matter what the outcome, if I lived or died, I would know that God was with me and in this moment, there was peace.

# STRENGTH IN WEAKNESS

There is strength in being weak. (1 Corinthians 12:10) Having peace in a situation no matter what the outcome is a place of victory. Jesus said something that on the face of it is strange.

*"And do not fear those who kill the body but cannot kill the soul. Rather fear him who can destroy both soul and body in hell." (Matthew 10:28, ESV)*

The context is not to worry about an enemy that can kill you. Keep on doing what God wants you to do no matter what happens because God is the one who controls your destination after the enemy has decimated you.

For me, that enemy was cancer ravaging my body. My body might have been broken and my spirit was close to being so, but once I realized that I didn't have to fear death I found a strength that I would not have believed possible if I didn't experience it.

I do not say this in arrogance or pride. Death is a horrible thing thing that was never intended for us by God. He wanted life and life abundantly. But when sin entered the world, death came with it.

Jesus shared in human life. Then he conquered death.

*"Since therefore the children share in flesh and blood, he himself likewise partook of the same things, that through death he might destroy the one who has the power of death, that is, the devil, and deliver all those who through fear of death were subject to lifelong slavery."*
*(Hebrews 2:14–15, ESV)*

The strength I found through brokenness was that of being set free from the subjection of death. The devil did this to me long ago, but all he had was fear. He had no substance. When that fear was removed, my spiritual muscles were flexed and the power to endure presented to me a way out. Brokenness equals strength equals endurance equals freedom.

Here are some practical steps that helped me battle against times of mental stress:

# YOU ARE NOT ALONE.

Realize that God, the source of life, has grace for you and that you are not alone. He has promised not to leave you and is near you in your frailty.

# REACH OUT TO A FRIEND.

Even Jesus, when in the most difficult time of his life in the garden, reached out to his best friends, Peter, John and James (Matthew 26:36-37).

# DO SOMETHING THAT MAKES YOU HAPPY.

*A merry heart makes a cheerful countenance, but by sorrow of the heart the spirit is broken. (Proverbs 15:13).*

In the first few months, my wife and I watched the television show, Frasier each night before bed. We laughed and laughed. It helped to keep our minds off of the most trying circumstances.

# EAT A HEALTHY DIET.

Elijah was depressed even to the point of death, then the Lord provided a good healthy meal—angel food cake! (See 1 Kings 19:6)

# GET SOME EXERCISE.

In 1 Kings 19:8, Elijah gets up and moves. He keeps going for days.

We should not look upon our weakness as a source of hopelessness, but of strength. It must be used as an opportunity to see the power of God work in and through us to have a positive impact on those around us. We have to be broken in order to be fixed. I am always excited to see a person encouraged or come to faith in Christ because of the most difficult time in my life. It makes it all worth it.

For certain people, humility is not enough. They need to see diplomas and letters after our name. My diplomas are an 88 staples scar running the length of my spine from T-10 to pelvic, scars stretching from my back to my belly, and the countless aches and pains I have endured. They are evidence of my education in brokenness.

But they are not what make me legit. Who does is the one who puts my broken pieces back together. I am approved by God for his work, to do his bidding either great or small, to change lives around the world. I find his approval in the precious blood of Jesus Christ! I am by no means as broken as I need to be, so he has work yet to do in me, but I am willing. Oh, God, I am wiling.

# 9.
# FINISHING WITH JOY
## PROCLAIMING THE GOSPEL OF GRACE

*Thinking about the finish line doesn't mean you are ready to stop running. It means that you have a goal in mind.*

# "IN A LITTLE TIME I MUST GO TO GOD. WHAT COMFORTS ME IN THIS LIFE IS THAT I NOW SEE HIM BY FAITH. I SEE HIM IN SUCH A MANNER AS MIGHT MAKE ME SAY SOMETIMES, I BELIEVE NO MORE, BUT I SEE. I FEEL WHAT FAITH TEACHES US,

# AND IN THAT ASSURANCE AND THAT PRACTICE OF FAITH I WILL LIVE AND DIE WITH HIM."

-Brother Lawrence (1)

Brother Lawrence was rounding the bend and could see the finish line up ahead. Things were beginning to make sense to him. He could see the course clearer and knew exactly what must be done in order to reach that line. His faith was slowly becoming sight. The sight of the finish line must have brought as much joy to Brother Lawrence as to the apostle Paul.

*"But none of these things move me; nor do I count my life dear to myself, so that I may finish my race with joy, and the ministry which I received from the Lord Jesus, to testify to the gospel of the grace of God." (Acts 20:24, NKJV)*

I want to be like this when I see the finish line. I don't know when that will be, but I do know that it will come. There will be a time that I will see the signs, hear the cheering and see the smiles. I have faith. I trust the Lord. My hope is to get to the point where my faith becomes so significant that it is as sight; and in that assurance, I practice faith and live and die with Christ.

# MY LIFE IS NOTHING IF NOT LIVED FOR CHRIST

As a senior pastor, life was good and crazy all at the same time. I learned the rhythm of it and learned to keep in stride, praying my way out of impossible situations and seeing the hand of the Lord at work. It was fun and stressful. It was fulfilling and yet sometimes devastating. Pastors need nerves of steel and an iron will or they will quickly leave the ministry out the back door. There needs to be a reason for serving in the ministry more than you are looking for a personal jet and 50,000-square-foot house. There has to be more to it than pats on the back and being the center of attention, which are things that can trip up pastors. They must have undoubting purpose of heart that tells them that they are called, no matter what comes their way.

That calling will be tested one way or another. It must be if the pastor will know whether they are truly called or not.

# WHAT MOVES ME?

The question is: What moves me? This is not a physical move. If that was the case, then cancer moved us from Fort Smith, Arkansas, to California. It means, what will get you to change course, literally a mind game.

For me, I had to answer two basic questions: Was I called? and Why am I questioning that call? When I was first diagnosed with cancer, it had the potential to completely take me out of ministry and derail the mission that God had me on. I could have shriveled up and died. But that is not the mission. The mission for me is the same as it has always been. I am to bear the name of Jesus, preach the gospel of grace and be willing to suffer for that glorious name.

That calling is not just for me, but for all of us. We have been called to bring the gospel to as many as will hear and to be willing to suffer for His name. Are you suffering? It was not given to destroy you, but to hone and to sharpen you that you might be a light-bearer.

# "PAINS AND SUFFERINGS WOULD BE A PARADISE TO ME WHILE I SUFFERED WITH MY GOD, AND THE GREATEST PLEASURES WOULD BE HELL TO ME IF I RELISHED THEM WITHOUT HIM. ALL MY CONSOLATION WOULD BE TO SUFFER SOMETHING FOR HIS SAKE." (2)

-Brother Lawrence

I can accomplish anything and go through any manner of suffering as long as I know that God is with me. But I am in a desperate darkness without him. If I am not confident of his leading I begin to get nervous. Will my pain have meaning? Or am I just suffering because of some stupid mistake I made? If God is with me, who can be against me? (Romans 8:31) But if God is not with me, there is no muscle, no might, no potentate nor power that can save me or give me courage!

# FINISHING MY RACE WELL

Keeping on mission can be very difficult. I tend to want easier tasks that give me a break or a breather. Perhaps this is sometimes important, but I was not called to live there. Finishing well is important. So many in the scriptures did not finish well. King Saul had great potential but ended up losing it all. Some of the great kings of Israel, like Jeroboam, the son of Nebat, had great potential but ultimately failed. Even good kings like Jehoshaphat and Hezekiah didn't finish well.

*"For I am already being poured out as a drink offering, and the time of my departure has come. I have fought the good fight, I have finished the race, I have kept the faith. Henceforth there is laid up for me the crown of righteousness, which the Lord, the righteous judge, will award to me on that day, and not only to me but also to all who have loved his appearing." (2 Timothy 4:6–8, ESV)*

The key to finishing well wasn't that the apostle was undoubting in his faith or that he had experienced peace and joy. It was because life was not about him. When I first heard the gospel I was amazed. Up to that point, religion had taught me to go to church on Sunday and when to stand or sit so that I wouldn't go to hell, but never introduced me to Jesus.

The Gospel was so different. I heard that my sins could be forgiven. I heard about Jesus, who loved me and died for me and even more, wanted a relationship with me. I wrote this chorus for a punk band I was in when I was 16 years old:

> *Jesus went all the way for you,*
> *What are you gonna do?*
> *Jesus went all the way for you,*
> *What are you gonna do? (3)*

The answer to these questions was: If Jesus went all the way for me, I was going to go all the way for him. I gave my life to Jesus Christ at that point so many years ago. My life is not my own. No matter how many times I try to take it back and really mess things up. During my most difficult moments I never really doubted God, nor did I ask why, but I did learn an intimacy with the Father that I never had before. And all these years later, the words that 16 year old wrote still haunt me. What am I going to do? Each time I attempt to take my life back,

# "JESUS WENT ALL THE WAY FOR YOU..."

One way to finish well is to be content. Contentedness is the antipathy of lust. Living a contented life is never easy, even though it is the right thing to do. I am not often in trouble when I am content. But discontentedness is the bane of the Spirit filled life. It transforms that one time commitment into a desire to fill my life with what will make me happy and not what God wants me to do with the life he has so graciously extended.

This is a problem for many of us who have survived life threatening situations. Some call it survivor's guilt. We have been spared. Now what? Why was I allowed to live and several of my friends have already received their eternal rewards? I know that I want to accomplish a great thing for God then I run into speed bumps on the way that slow my enthusiasm. Then I condemn myself for not doing what I am supposed to be doing. I am just as called to serve God as a cancer survivor as I was before cancer. What if God's point in saving me was not for some grand purpose, although I pray that many are reached through this book you are reading, but perhaps it is that God wanted me to live my life doing what he has always called me to do until the calling changes and I stand in his presence in perfect contentedness. I long to hear the words from the lips of the Savior, Well done, good and faithful servant!" (Matthew 25:23)

## LIFE IS NOT DEAR

When our life is our own, we want the comforts of this world. We are no longer content with the things of God. However, when our life, our creature comforts, our self-preservation is not important to us, we are free. What someone is willing to die for says a lot about them. It displays the most important thing in life. Soldiers lay down their lives for their country. Suicide bombers are willing to lay down their lives for an ideology. Others are willing to give their lives for love.

*For when we were still without strength, in due time Christ died for the ungodly. For scarcely for a righteous man will one die; yet perhaps for a good man someone would even dare to die. But God demonstrates His own love toward us, in that while we were still sinners, Christ died for us (Romans 5:6–8).*

The point is that if Christ was willing to die for us, then we should be willing to lay down our lives for him. This doesn't mean that we actually kill ourselves for the cause. But it does mean that if we had to choose between this life and the next, then we are willing to choose the next. And not only that, but to take as many people to heaven, through the preaching of the gospel of grace, as possible.

# WHAT DOES IT TAKE TO FINISH THE RACE?

The measure of finishing well is that I had a changed life. Becoming a pastor was a big change, a choice I had to make. But now, during this cancer battle, it would appear that I don't have a choice.

On the other hand, I did have a choice. Years ago, I made the choice to give my life to Christ, and in doing so, I made the choice that whatever came my way, sickness or health, I was going to be a child of God and follow him until the day I see him face to face. The preparation for a difficult life was to surrender my heart to Christ, before the difficulties came. Then, when they did, He was able to make me strong enough to endure even the most trying storm.

There was a violent overthrow of the kingdom of Israel by the Babylonians. Society as they knew it had been demolished as the foreign army occupied the territory. Daniel and his friends, who were part of the royal family, were spared and taken to Babylon for re-education. They received a college degree in the Babylonian language, culture and art. Finally, it came time to be presented before the great king, Nebuchadnezzar for evaluation. Their teacher found out that Daniel and his friends were not eating the food that was given to them from the king, but were only eating vegetables. Even though they were young, they wanted to honor their God by eating a kosher diet. After a time of testing, these Hebrew children were actually healthier looking that those who had eaten the delicacies of the king. Nebuchadnezzar accepted them with eager anticipation of what they would do for the Empire.

They determined to honor God so that whatever came their way, their decision would be firm regardless of the consequences. They would have joy in knowing their God, rather than the difficulty of having to make the decision on the fly. If I had to make the decision to follow Christ when cancer struck, I probably would not have been able to endure.

## WITH JOY

There is no way out of the darkness of facing the battles of cancer, financial troubles, the loss of a job, or even enduring the loss of a child or spouse without a little joy. Joy brings light into an otherwise dark, overwhelming emotional crisis. I learned early on that if I wanted to finish well, I would have to do it with joy. To do so would require me to stay on mission and remembering that I will not be moved by any circumstance that comes my way. The decision was made long ago. I am still here. I must continually re-focus and realize how joyful a life serving Jesus can be!

These are nice things to say, but how can I live them? Believe me, I have been confronted on many occasions regarding the goodness of God. I was diagnosed with cancer. How is this the goodness of God? I soon could not afford to pay the bills. How is this the goodness of God? I know people who's wives and children have died. How is this the goodness of God?

*"My God, Thou has helped me to see, that whatever good be in honor and rejoicing, how good is he who give them, and can withdraw them; that blessedness does not lie so much in receiving good from and in thee, but in holding forth thy glory and virtue;*

*that it is an amazing thing to see Deity in creature, speaking acting, filling, shining through it; that I am near good when I am near Thee, that to be like Thee is a glorious thing: This is my magnet, my attraction"(4)*
*-Brother Lawrence*

The goodness of God is not in what God gives or take away, but in how He works in us. I am not saying that God is good because He paid all my bills and healed me and my family or allowed me to get a new job. I am saying that God is good because He got me through the loss of all these things. His goodness is shown in my weakness and my response to it.

# "WHATEVER REMEDIES YOU MAKE USE OF, THEY WILL SUCCEED ONLY SO FAR AS HE PERMITS. WHEN PAINS COME FROM GOD, HE ONLY CAN CURE THEM. HE OFTEN SENDS DISEASES OF THE BODY TO CURE THOSE OF THE SOUL. COMFORT YOURSELF WITH THE SOVEREIGN PHYSICIAN OF THE SOUL AND BODY." (5)

-Brother Lawrence

Therefore, the key to finishing the race is the joy that we experience through the fact that life on earth is not as real as life in heaven. That is reality, this is just the shadow. The more we connect to this world, the less heaven will seem important to us, and vise-versa. And yet, when heaven is our hope, disease and difficulty become our special friends leading us to a glorious end!

*"When Alexander the Great was preparing to leave Macedonia for the conquest of Persia, he gave all his goods to his faithful friends and servants. Peridiccas, one of his favorites, asked the king what he had reserved for himself, and he answered that he had reserved hope. If ours is the hope, as a sure and unmovable anchor within the veil then we shall die well" (6)*

If we want to die well, we must live as if the only thing we possess is the hope found in the everlasting gospel of Jesus Christ and the mission we have been given—to share that gospel with as many people as possible, without regard to our own comforts or desires.

As I write this, I am thinking of how one of my friends met his end. He worshipped the Lord, witnessed to people and brought at least one person to Christ from his sick-bed in the last two-weeks of his life before he took his last breath. When he opened his eyes in glory, he heard those wonderful words: "Well done, good and faithful servant." That is what I long to hear, and how I want to pass to heaven.

# WHOSE MINISTRY IS IT?
## THE MINISTRY IS FROM THE LORD

The mission I am on came from Christ and he will fulfill it in me. I didn't start it, and I won't be the one to finish it in my own strength. I am confident that he will complete the work. He called me to do my portion and equipped me to complete the task. I am indestructible until I have carried out his orders, conversely, I won't be here one second longer once the mission is complete.

*For to me, to live is Christ, and to die is gain. But if I live on in the flesh, this will mean fruit from my labor; yet what I shall choose I cannot tell. For I am hard-pressed between the two, having a desire to depart and be with Christ, which is far better. Nevertheless to remain in the flesh is more needful for you (Philippians 1:21–24).*

Paul was very conflicted. He longed to be with Jesus, but he was also wanting to finish the mission.

This is how all those who suffer should act. The writer of the Hebrews wrote:

For those who say such things declare plainly that they seek a homeland. And truly if they had called to mind that country from which they had come out, they would have had opportunity to return. But now they desire a better, that is, a heavenly country. Therefore God is not ashamed to be called their God, for He has prepared a city for them
(Hebrews 11:14–16).

Making the decision to be on mission, not worrying about our own lives, gives us the strength to run our race with joy.

# FREEDOM IN BEING A SERVANT

I am free when I am a servant. I don't have to make things up as I go along. I receive from the Lord and give what I have been given to others. Surrendering my life to Christ was the best thing I ever did. It made me into an ambassador for Christ bringing a message of hope for this life and for the next, the everlasting gospel of grace.

# THE MOST IMPORTANT PART OF LIFE

It has been said that G.R.A.C.E. means "God's Riches At Christ's Expense."

I did not just receive grace, but grace upon grace as God's gift to me. How can I be proud of achieving something that has been given to me and that I had no participation in earning? Grace in the New Testament is usually coupled with mercy. Grace is getting what what we don't deserver; mercy, not getting what we do deserve. Grace provides the riches of Christ, mercy keeps us from the judgment that we so earnestly deserve. Where we tend to fall short is that we have a high opinion of ourselves and want to earn our way through life and eventually to the after-life. If we continue in that vein, then we will never attain that which we think we'll earn, but if we surrender, then every longing of the heart to know God will be ours to the glory of God and for our good. It is an amazing, if a bit backwards, plan of action that removes sin and rebellion and gives us an eternal home with our Creator, Father and Friend.

Imagine an ISIS terrorist who hates the United States of America. He is doing everything to thwart the plans of the country. Then the president decides that there will be forgiveness, and even citizenship, for any terrorist who wishes to renounce ISIS and come and live in the United States. Of course, everyone would be suspect. The terrorist would have a hard time believing that all the benefits of citizenship would be given to him; and the people of the country would be concerned that it wasn't a true conversion.

This was the story of the apostle Paul, who had been arresting and condemning Christians. He was doing everything he could to stop the Kingdom of God from expanding. Then God confronted him with amazing grace! At the beginning, people didn't believe that he had truly converted. They were afraid he was trying to get close to them to kill them. But it was true. God had extended grace and mercy to this former terrorist. So how could he do anything other than tell everyone he could about what God had done? That is why I have a commitment to the gospel of grace. It is powerful and changes lives. It is the only message we have. It declares the goodness of God in the lives of those touched by it.

My testimony is that I am a sinner saved by grace. I was attempting to be "good enough" and found that even religion could not help. But when I met Jesus it all changed! I am changed. His grace is amazing and abounding in me.

Sure, I am battling Stage 4 cancer. Yes, God has done amazing things in me. I had three major surgeries and one minor surgery in four months. I have metal in my back holding my spine together, which have now snapped, where the cancer had eaten through my vertebrae. I have had three bouts with cancer and survived them all so far. I should not be walking or able to do what I do. But that is not my testimony. I testify of the gospel of grace because He saved me. The fact that Jesus died on the cross and rose on the third day means that I will be with Him forever and ever one day. Therefore, I do not lose hope.

Is something moving you today? Perhaps you don't know the Savior. Then it is my mission to tell you that He loves you. His desire is to give you hope in this world and in the next. You might be suffering now without reason and hope. With Christ you have a friend who understands what you are going through and can help in time of need.

If you want to know Jesus today, it is very simple, even though a profound thing happens inside of you. The Bible tells us that if we confess with our mouth the Lord Jesus and believe in our hearts that God has raised Him from the dead, we will be saved. It means that we must understand that Jesus is Lord. He is the one who is in charge, the boss. Rising from the dead means that He died on the cross for our sins and then rose again on the third day. The cross tells us that we are sinners and that we need a Savior, otherwise, Jesus would not have had to suffer and die for those sins. Therefore, if you know that you are not righteous (a sinner) and in need of a Savior (a champion to fight sin on your behalf), and believe that He is alive after being raised from the dead, then you are saved.

At this point, it would be a great idea to pray and give your life into the hands of the God who loves you. Pray that prayer that comes from your heart, something like this:

God, I know that I am a sinner in need of a Savior. Be my Lord and Savior. I give you my life, save me and forgive me. I turn away from the old life of sin with your help and ask that you would be my strength all of my days. In Jesus name, Amen.

Congratulations! Welcome to the family of God. Tell someone about your decision to follow Christ. Get into a good, Bible-teaching church so you can be encouraged in your new relationship with your heavenly Father.
May the Lord bless and heal you.

# 10.
# AS GOOD AS OUR LAST SCAN
## FIGHTING CANCER IN THE SPIRIT

*"As cold water to a weary soul, So is good news from a far country." (Proverbs 25:25, NKJV)*

*"For the righteous will never be moved; he will be remembered forever. He is not afraid of bad news; his heart is firm, trusting in the Lord." (Psalm 112:6–7, ESV)*

We are only as good as our last scan. Every cancer patient will understand this. It does not matter if you have been cancer-free for years. Each and every time you go into the CT or the MRI, you are thinking that this may be the time that you find that the cancer is back. I know people who have felt this way after being cancer free for ten years or more. It is just what happens. It is a fear that each one of us have to live with.

But for me, for years, the results were nothing more than information. It did not matter if the results came back that I had a massive tumor or that the cancer had spread throughout my lungs. It was only information. Information that had to be acted upon. Cancer medication after cancer medication had worked... until it didn't. When my chemo pills stopped working, the answer was not to throw up my hands in fear, but to find out what the next treatment was going to be. Was it a new pill? Was it immunotherapy? Was it something else? There was always something else.

It is much easier for me to think of test results as "information" in order to allow my brain to function rather than my heart. Emotions can lead to depths of darkness of which there is no return. A good attitude and control of emotions are essential to ensuring that there would be another treatment and another drug, and that it would work.

# HE WILL WIPE AWAY EVERY TEAR FROM THEIR EYES, AND DEATH SHALL BE NO MORE

Don't get me wrong, I had known other cancer patients who had exhausted their regimen. They had been told there was something else they could try—a clinical trial; a new treatment; a pill. These treatments worked... until they didn't. They knew their Savior and I can only imagine the joy they felt when they heard him say, "Well done, good and faithful servant." Their pain was gone, their fight was over and their hope fulfilled, yes, fulfilled. Their hope was never in the next drug or treatment, but in living a life that glorified their Liberator; their Champion; Jesus, who gave them their final treatment which infused life in them that exclaimed to the pale rider that this one was Christ's, and that their healing was complete.

*"And I heard a loud voice from the throne saying, "Behold, the dwelling place of God is with man. He will dwell with them, and they will be his people, and God himself will be with them as their God. He will wipe away every tear from their eyes, and death shall be no more, neither shall there*

*be mourning, nor crying, nor pain anymore, for the former*
*things have passed away."" (Revelation 21:3–4)*

I was told that I had one last treatment and if that did not work, then I had reached the end of what human beings could provide. Of course there are other treatments that are extremely dangerous and even deadly, but of those that offered some semblance of hope, the end had been reached. This news, this "information", was a different experience. After years of chemotherapy and even a clinical trial that helped destroy 90% of the tumors in my lungs, I had finally heard those words that cancer patients dread. But was this too, just information?

In August of 2019 I was given hope that I had not expected. Previously, I had been told that the tumor in my lung, an aggressive monster we called, "The Beast," was inoperable. I was still receiving immunotherapy, but it just wasn't enough to kill that belligerent tumor.

At a later oncology appointment, I was told that I was now able to have an operation to remove, "the Beast." The surgery was set for August 29, 2019. The lower lobe of my right lung, along with the tumor that was terrorizing my body, was removed. It felt good to have it gone and I had energy that I had not experienced in years, but it only lasted a few months. I started to get fatigued again.

I was asked to speak at our home church for both the main services and for the youth the following week. After speaking to the youth, I began to feel extremely fatigued. It came on quickly, faster than I would have expected. I could feel death in me again. I sensed that perhaps the cancer was back.

Scans done in December revealed that I had a 2.6cm tumor growing in my sacrum. At an oncology appointment I was told that the immunotherapy had stopped working and that I should stop getting infused. However, the oncologist asked if I had ever taken Afinitor, an mTor inhibitor, which I had not. He informed me that this would be my last chance before more complicated and deadly treatments would be discussed.

For weeks I had not been able to sleep in a bed because of pain in my lower back. The only sleep I was getting was while leaning against a wall or sitting in a chair. My sleep was broken and I would wake up in pain. I also began feeling sleep deprived, not just exhausted. A week after my oncology appointment, I experienced severe pain and went to the Emergency Department at our local hospital. They gave me pain medication and kept me for observation and released me hours later. I remember feeling confused and even a little embarrassed that I "wasted" their time.

# THE WORSE PAIN I HAD EVER EXPERIENCED

The next day, I was still in bad pain, especially toward the evening. At this point, my brother-in-law was fighting for his life, getting a heart transplant after months in the hospital with his wife at his side. Monica, and I were watching their daughter, Jordyn while my sister-in-law was with him in the hospital. Jordyn was asleep with Monica in our room and I was in the front room leaning against a wall, trying to sleep. I could not sleep at all; the pain was intense and getting worse. I was completely sleep deprived and ready to faint after almost a month of little to no sleep. I remember praying that God would heal me and that I could get some sleep. The prayers were in earnest as my eyes filled with tears.

The living room has a dining area that transitioned into a living room with a puffy lazy-boy recliner, a couch and a love-seat set up in an "L" shape, then a TV that can be watched from the seated position on either the couch, love-seat or the recliner. I hobbled toward the recliner from the dinning area using a walker. I was more tired than I had ever been. I positioned myself and the walker where I had my back toward the recliner and slowly lowered myself toward the edge of the soft area of the recliners seat. It felt good to sit and then, I was asleep.

I woke up screaming in agony! I heard what sounded like a pop in my groin, then excruciating, blinding pain; the worse I had ever felt up to that point in my life. I was screaming and I cried out for God to help me and for Monica to call 911. She burst out of the bedroom, which is just off the dining area, and my poor, 7-year-old niece awoke due to the loud yelling. My wife asked what was wrong and I screeched and wailed and through the whoops got out the words, 9-1-1! I was in horrible blinding hot pain and was stuck in the position I was on the recliner, unable to move. She called 911 and within minutes, paramedics and the fire department arrived. I was still bawling with tears streaming down my furled face.

The first thought of the firemen and paramedics was to lift me up off the lazy-boy, but just their touch sent me into horror. I asked if they would grab my hands and pull me up to a standing position. When they did, I experienced lightning pain, again tears poured from my eyes to accompany the screams and unutterable prayers. Once I was able to calm down a bit, I noticed that the pain did dull in the standing position. I felt a bit better. In the hospital, to determine the level of pain, there is a chart on the wall that shows what kind of face best describes your pain. Under each face beginning with a happy face, ending with a frown and tears was a number from 1 to 10. Believe it or not, I knew from previous surgeries that they would be asking me what level my pain was. My first thought was a sledge hammer pounding the smiley face until it was reduced to lines and even powder, and that would begin to touch the surface of the pain I had experienced. But now, the pain had subsided and now it was reduced to somewhere between 9 and 10.

I reached forward to grab the walker that one of the firefighters had put in front of me and steadied myself. With this much pain, I would be headed for the hospital soon, but that meant I would have to get on a stretcher and take a ride in the back of an ambulance. When I walked around the recliner, I reached the stretcher and noticed that the two paramedics had tears in their eyes at my pain. They made the stretcher as low as they could and attempted to help me to sit and then lay down on it. I tried the first time and I was back at the sledgehammer pain! At this, the paramedics helped me to stand quickly and relieve the pain. I sat once again and felt only a slight amount of pain, they seized the opportunity and strapped me in and placed me in the back of the ambulance. Then, during the ride (without lights and sirens), even stopping at red lights, I was screaming once again in horrid pain.

I arrived at the emergency department and was wheeled into the triage area, which, at this time of night, was a hallway as I waited for an exam room. I asked the paramedic that was with me if I could stand for a moment. He was reluctant, but eventually he let me get up and the pain subsided. I was later given a massive amount of pain medication and was admitted into the hospital and stayed under their care for 10 days as they struggled to figure out what caused the pain. They scheduled an MRI. I had to be placed under anesthesia to do so and when I awoke, they lifted me up immediately to stop the pain. When I met with my oncologist, he told me that the 2.6cm tumor was now 7.6cm. "The Beast" was back! It had revived and was now living in my sacrum! While in the hospital I was given doses of radiation, my radiation oncologist believed that he could kill the tumor, and perhaps, alleviate my pain, but there was one caveat—I had to do it sitting up because of the pain. This actually seemed to excite the physicists in the office. It was a challenge and they looked forward to solving the problem.

I was released from the hospital toward the last few treatments and I was able to ring the bell. During this time, I had sent the images and reports to my neurosurgeon, Dr. Shafizadeh in Arkansas. He called and wanted Monica to take a video of me walking. He called back after he received it and the records from my radiation oncologist and the hospital and told me that I needed a brace as soon as possible because what the doctors here didn't tell me was that the rods on both sides of my spine were "fractured" at L2 and L3, just below the cage and this could be the cause of my pain for which I would need surgery immediately. There wasn't even a question, the only person to ever do surgery on my back was Dr. Shafizadeh and he would be the only one that would do it now. I would need to go back to Arkansas.

During my stay in the hospital, I started my chemo regimen of Afinitor. Due to the radiation treatments, my legs started to swell up to twice of what is normal. Even after I came home from the hospital I could not sleep in a bed because of the pain. I slept in a chair and put my feet up on a leg rest. If the tumor in the sacrum was the source of the pain and not the rods, then I would be okay, if not, then I would need some pain medication until I was able to have surgery and beyond. We made an appointment with a palliative care doctor who prescribed some medications that helped keep the pain to a minimum. During this time I went through all sorts of emotions. I felt fear and sadness. I was opposed to palliative care because it seemed so final.

I had heard that people who entered palliative or Hospice care did so at the dying stage of life. I didn't sense that I was there yet, so I resisted. Later I found that this sort of care, especially palliative, was not just for people who were just about to die, but were available for those in an immense amount of pain, like I was. I acquiesced. This was not an admission of defeat, but an ability to continue to function in daily life.

I was fearful of what a flight from California to Arkansas would be like and if I would experience the pain that I had experienced just weeks earlier. The LORD provided some wonderful friends who had airline miles that they were willing to use to fly us first class (a luxury we would never normally be able to have) so that I could hopefully be in a position of least pain if the pain returned. The food wasn't that bad either. My legs were still swollen and I began feeling some pressure as we lifted up from the runway at John Wayne Airport in Orange County, but nothing too bad. I prayed and prayed that nothing would happen, and, praise God, nothing did. We landed in Fort Smith, Arkansas, where we own a home and where our three adult sons live. It was a joy to see them. Within a few days, we rented a vehicle and went for my appointment with Dr. Shafizadeh in the Little Rock area and went through an MRI and CT scan in preparation for surgery.

From the hotel I called to confirm if we had to be there at 5am or if we had to arrive a half-hour earlier because it wasn't quite clear. When I spoke to scheduling, they said that I was not scheduled. I told them that I was just with the doctor and had tests and was prepped. They still said that I was not on the schedule. The next morning I called my doctor's office and they said that Dr. Shafizadeh wanted to see me. We met later that morning. He showed me the MRI and CT scans. What I thought were "fractures," hairline weaknesses in the metal, were actually breaks and the two rods were separated from each other. I was unable to get my brace in California, but I made sure I got it soon after this meeting! My doctor explained to me that the position of the tumor, which had now either grown or was the same size, was in a difficult place to have surgery. The surgery to replace the rods could happen, but there was another problem. My white and red blood cells were VERY low and I would probably die on the operating table in the process, or the procedure would not help in any way. The surgery was too dangerous to proceed at this time, but he would work with my oncologist in Fort Smith to get me ready for surgery by boosting my white and red blood cells with medication.

# A REASON FOR THE MESS

*"And we know that for those who love God all things work together for good, for those who are called according to his purpose." (Romans 8:28)*

I left feeling a little strange. I was puzzled and asked Monica, "Why did we come all the way here to be told that the reason why we are here cannot happen?" We were not sure and prayed and asked the Lord the same question. There had to be some reason we traveled all the way across the country to Arkansas.

We returned to our Fort Smith home. By this time, the United States had closed down due to CoVid-19 and it was impossible to travel, even within the country, without rigorous rules to follow, so we decided to stay and see if my oncologist there could figure out how I could get the surgery I needed. At my first appointment with him he asked me what chemo I was on. I told him Afinator. He said that it worked best with another drug called Lenvima, even though it was a "nasty" drug that had bad side-effects. I started taking that drug and, true to form, after a month, I was experienced very high blood pressure. It was a rough time, but I did my best, being prescribed blood pressure medicine. Every few weeks I was given shots to increase my white blood cell production to no avail.

During this time, the swelling in my legs turned into large large blisters called Cellulitis which were painful and could be deadly. My doctor in Arkansas prescribed home-health for me which would come and change my bandages and would monitor my progress.

After months of attempting to get ready for surgery, it was called off for good. There was no way I would survive the surgery. I thought about why I would come all the way across the country to get a surgery that would eventually be called off.

In June, Monica, her dad and I went on a mini-vacation to a town in the Ozark mountains of Arkansas about an hour drive away called Eureka Springs. The town has a mountain village feel and is very artsy. Its claim to fame is its Passion Play, Bible Lands, a life-size Tabernacle, Biblical Art and Bible Museums. While looking at my favorite thing of all, The Word of God at the Bible Museum, I began speaking with a couple from Texas. We hit it off quickly and started to talk about life and our walks with the Lord including my battle with cancer. Connected to the Museum was the book store, where we purchased tickets for the Bible Lands tour which allowed us to see the Tabernacle, some first century dwellings and feed some camels along the way.

# "WE REBUKE CANCER IN THE NAME OF JESUS,"

It was a hot day, and since I was fatigued, it took me a little longer to get back from the tour. In fact, we were the last ones on the walkway when we noticed there was a couple waiting under the arches of a giant first-century gate and wall. It was the couple we had met earlier at the Bible Museum, Rennard and Kim. They told us that they were waiting until we returned so they could pray for me. Monica and I were shocked and told them that we would be more than happy to be prayed for. It was a powerful, Spirit-filled time of prayer. I remember some of his words that day, "We rebuke cancer in the name of Jesus," and, "I curse cancer in the name of Jesus," and "my brother is a child of God, Your property, O God, and therefore, this cancer cannot live in him," and, "in the name of Jesus, cancer be gone!"

Now, I was raised charismatic and to believe that all the gifts are for today, but when someone prays like this there is always some skepticism. Are they correct in what they are assuming? Is it okay to pray this way? Is this how Christians are supposed to pray? There are those who are charismatic and there are those who are CHARISMATIC! I have been prayed for several times over the years. Some, who are supposed to believe in supernatural healing have prayed like this, "Father, Steve is sick, we want him to get better, but if

You want to take him home, that's okay with us as well. We don't really need him to get better, unless You want him to be so. Amen." Then I have been prayed for by those who say things that they truly don't believe, but they pray it anyway because that is what they are supposed to pray, "Lord, we command you to heal our brother! You must do it. You have to do it!" When people pray like this for me, I almost want to step out of the way of the lightning bolt that may be coming in from heaven. I definitely pray with my eyes open with these people. Then there are prayers like Rennard prayed. He not only had a system of beliefs that he held to, a sort of faith led belief, but he believed with all his heart. His was different. I would most assuredly rather be prayed for by someone like Rennard, than someone that wants the Lord to kill me on the spot!

There was something eye-opening and precious about being prayed for by this man, a tall black man who looked to be in his late thirties. The Holy Spirit moved in him powerfully and I could feel something happening, something different. What that was, I was not sure, but it was certainly good. We parted ways and the next day, we left to return back to Fort Smith.

At an oncology appointment I asked about scans to see my progress. They were scheduled for July 22. After the scans I asked for a copy of the discs, which I picked up a few days later. Monica had traveled with her dad to her cousin's home in Oklahoma when I received the discs. I put them in my Mac and fired up the app to read the scans. Dr. Shafizadeh, my neurosurgeon, taught me years earlier how to read the scans, so I began looking to see how large the tumor in my sacrum had grown, or, hopefully, had shrunk, and if the tumors in my lungs had shrunk at all. I looked two, three, four times, then again and again. I couldn't believe what I was seeing and I attributed it to my lack of ability to read the scans. I called Monica and told her, also saying I would call the hospital and ask them for the report to be sent to me so I could confirm what I was seeing. They told me that the report was ready and could be found on my app. It confirmed it. They could not find any active cancer in my body at all! It was a miracle. It was impossible.

The report read,

# "STABLE EXAM WITH NO EVIDENCE OF METASTATIC DISEASE."

After battling stage 4 cancer for 6 years, all that time in treatment, I, for the first time in 3 years had received information that said that I had no NO ACTIVE CANCER in my body!

# PRAISE GOD!

I don't like to be negative, nor doubt the Lord, but I do want to rejoice in what He has done up to this point. Our ministry exists to minister to people who have lost hope in this world and in the next. We want to tell them that there is hope in both. When I get another scan; remember, cancer patients are only as good as their last scan, if that scan comes back with tumors, then that too is just information that needs to be acted on. Will it be a disappointment? Of course, I am human. However, with the time that God has given me, and with the energy, being filled with his power and strength, I want to do His will and tell as many as possible that Jesus has given us hope and because of His cross, we can have life everlasting! Amen .

# NOTES

Chapter 3

1. https://www.nimh.nih.gov/health/statistics/any-anxiety-disorder.shtml
2. https://www.nimh.nih.gov/health/statistics/major-depression.shtml
3. https://www.who.int/news-room/fact-sheets/detail/depression
4. https://www.cdc.gov/tobacco/campaign/tips/diseases/depression-anxiety.html
5. https://www.nimh.nih.gov/health/statistics/suicide.shtml
   a) https://www.cdc.gov/nchs/fastats/suicide.htm
   b) https://www.who.int/mental_health/prevention/suicide/suicideprevent/en/


Chapter 6

1. Charles Haddon Spurgeon
2. Allan C. Emery, A Turtle on a Fencepost (Waco, TX: Word Books 1979), 53. Quoted in, Robert J.

Morgan, The Lord Is My Shepherd (Simon & Schuster, 2013), 50-51.

Chapter 8

1. Reference page: Theology Learned in the Flames of Adversity. https://www.ligonier.org/blog/theology-learned-flames-adversity/
2. Charles Haddon Spurgeon

Chapter 9

1. Brother Lawrence,
2. Brother Lawrence,
3. Steve Marquez, UAO
(Jesus Went All The Way For You, 1988)
4. The Valley of Vision, The All-Good
5. Brother Lawrence
6. Herbert Lockyer, Last Words of Saints and Sinners